BEYOND THE FIRST DANCE

Phil –
Linda wants you
to read this !

Susan

Beyond the First Dance

A Guide for Couples to Think Beyond their Wedding Day

Susan McKeown, APRN, CPS

STAYING-IN-SYNC PUBLISHING
Manchester, New Hampshire

Composed in Minion Pro at Hobblebush Design
www.hobblebush.com

Printed in the United States of America

ISBN: 978-0-9961902-0-6
Library of Congress Control Number: 2015905123

STAYING-IN-SYNC PUBLISHING
299 Steinmetz Drive
Manchester, New Hampshire 03104

This book is dedicated to my beloved husband, Patrick,
without whom this endeavor would not have been possible.
Thank you for your love, respect, support and
encouragement of my dreams.

Contents

Section Two: "The Tango"

THE PASSION OF THE EARLY YEARS OF MARRIAGE

Acknowledgments

I WOULD LIKE TO ACKNOWLEDGE Dr. Paul Ashton for allowing me and my husband the privilege of speaking with engaged couples over these many years. My appreciation goes to my college friends, Kathy, Linda, Lucille, Pamela and Tina for their encouragement in following "one's heart's desire." Thanks to my Book Club for permitting me to remain an honorary member while I pursued my writing. Special appreciation goes to college classmates, Paul and Kathleen Casey and Dr. John Buchino, and my dear friend, Marcy Lyman, for your enthusiasm and helpful suggestions reviewing the manuscript. Sincere gratitude to Herb Pence, Kathy Fortin, Joanne Lahiff and Rosamond Van Der Linden, my devoted writer's group, for their continued, unfailing feedback during our sessions. You are definitely the "write" team! To all my friends and my neighbor, Carol Gayman, for the encouragement given over the many years of pulling this book together. The help from Dawn O'Connor and Joe Gallagher with computer skills and formatting was invaluable. And finally to my husband, Patrick, and our now grown children, Katie and her husband, Chris, Eileen, Daniel and Matthew for all the material you provided by sharing your views and opinions, and just for being the people whom I love.

—S.M.

Preface

"WHO HERE IS PLANNING ON GETTING DIVORCED?"
Sitting in front of me are forty engaged couples, mostly in
their late twenties, who have made the decision to attend a
seven-hour seminar in preparation for their upcoming marriage. The only hand that goes up is my husband Patrick's,
which adds levity to the quiet room. After forty-plus years of
marriage, I tell him that ship has sailed, and the couples laugh.
Even though they paid to take this day-long course, they must
be questioning why they forfeited a beautiful Sunday afternoon, while they sit on cold, metal chairs, in a church hall,
listening to strangers the age of their parents.

What husband and wife to-be anticipate that their marriage will end in divorce? No one I have met, and certainly
none of the optimistic, passionate, bright, young faces staring
back at me. Statistics, however, show that roughly one-half
of all marriages today are headed in that direction. As an
Advanced Practice Registered Nurse (APRN), I have worked
with families for over forty years and have witnessed the devastation of fractured relationships for far too many couples.
"Gray divorces" (couples over fifty) currently have the highest
rate! What happens? Are there issues that, if addressed early
on, could ensure a better chance for a satisfying, long-term
marriage? Patrick and I believe there are or we would not
have given up our precious Sunday afternoon either!

Forty-four years ago, Patrick and I attended a "Pre-Cana
Seminar," before being married in our church. We went

under duress, arrived late and sat in the last row with our arms crossed in defiance. We gazed at our watches while the speakers prattled on about topics we apparently thought were irrelevant. This group appears much more polite and receptive, and I commend them for investing this time in their relationship and forthcoming marriage. Indeed, their decision to seek premarital education and counseling has shown to result in higher marriage satisfaction and to lessen the likelihood of divorce. An article by Po Bronson and Ashley Merryman entitled, "Will This Marriage Last?" (Time.com, June 30, 2006) states, "Couples who have attended premarital classes or counseling cut their odds of divorce by almost a third. We don't know if the classes actually change the couples, or if those couples are already realistic and savvy to the dangers which is why they were smart enough to take the class." The authors go on to add, "Premarital counseling might be the best wedding gift any newlyweds can receive." I believe that what couples learn about themselves during such sessions are lessons they can draw on for years to come.

During our session with the couples, we address the group on the topics of communication, finances and spirituality, because these, along with sex and in-laws, are the leading causes in the dissolution of marriages. The couples then have the opportunity to talk to each other on these topics. It is hoped that raising the issues beforehand will help these marriages succeed, thus lowering the likelihood of divorce. Too often, couples have placed this program last on their premarital bucket list, attending just weeks before getting married. With the wedding date imminent, it is unlikely there will be time to address these important issues with the depth they deserve. The financial commitment that has been made for their special day precludes any discussion that might put this event in jeopardy.

Looking at the faces of these couples, it is evident that love is in the air and that is good! It is just that their timing for attending this program is not ideal. This realization is what led to my writing this book. In a perfect world, couples should be exploring these topics before they make the decision to get engaged. As anyone who has been engaged knows, once the engagement is announced and the date is set, the focus is on wedding planning. The couple must secure the location for the ceremony, reserve the reception site, invite their wedding party and guests, select the attire, choose music and flowers, plan for accommodations and limousines, determine honeymoon destination and attend to the myriad of particulars to make this a "once in a lifetime" celebration. All these details require a financial commitment. It then becomes a considerable investment of money, time and energy. Very little, if any, thought is given to life after the big day, namely, the marriage. Since these couples are usually within three months of their wedding, it is not the ideal time to introduce the leading causes of marital friction. It would be in their best interest to talk about these prior to their engagement.

When a couple is dating, they are usually working full-time or pursing higher education, perhaps even both simultaneously. Sometimes they are geographically separated. The work week is filled with anticipation of spending time together. Weekends are treasured time for relaxing, enjoying outdoor activities, a romantic dinner and talking about future plans and dreams. No one wants to break the spell with topics that might lead to arguments. Controversy is not wanted during this time that is filled with passion and prognostications. That can wait until later, they may think.

Exactly, when is later? This period of serious dating is the most appropriate time to experience each other in many different situations. This book covers a number of topics which should be addressed early in a relationship, before making any commitment to an engagement: engaging in activities with each other's families and friends and discussions about religion, education and politics, to name a few. It is a time to witness the other's beliefs, attitudes and opinions in different settings and circumstances and get a strong sense of each other's values.

Once engaged, these formerly free, fun-filled, forty-eight-hour weekends are often cut short, attending to the earlier mentioned pre-wedding activities. Their brief time together allows the couple no real chance to discuss the issues that will need to be addressed during their married life. The focus has shifted. Granted, some aspects of planning a wedding provide opportunities for compromise, discussion of finances and learning about each other's likes and dislikes, as they buy furniture, decide on housing and choose a honeymoon destination. It just makes it much more stressful if the couple were then to decide it would be better to delay, postpone or cancel their plans to marry. To do so is financially costly and emotionally embarrassing to family and friends. So is divorce!

Surveying 13,000 couples in 2013, TheKnot.com found the average cost of a wedding in the United States was $29, 858.00, not including the honeymoon. The average cost of a divorce is estimated at $20,000.00 from Theweddingreport.com. The real fee will vary depending on where you live, the assets involved and how long the process takes. Many people reading this know that both these events are often much more costly. These figures do not take into account the emotional devastation of divorce. Such expenditures should be taken seriously when a couple is considering marriage. Deciding to postpone or cancel a wedding is not an easy thing to do, but it may be the wisest, if either party is at all hesitant about the decision.

Fortunate is the couple that has not yet set a date and

entangled themselves with monetary obligations. They are free to discuss the subjects that will inevitably come up in their future, if they decide on marriage. They have the opportunity to address their differences, have honest dialogue, learn how to compromise and identify issues that may need more discussion. They have the freedom to decide that some things pose such an impediment that perhaps they should not move forward with an engagement. Not easy, but ask anyone who has gone through a divorce, which they would choose?

As a Certified Prevention Specialist (CPS), I encourage being proactive. It is less physically and emotionally costly to prevent undesirable circumstances than it is to change them later. In this book there are a number of topics which should be addressed early in a relationship, before making any commitment to an engagement: the importance of knowing yourself, recognizing those qualities that could pose a danger to your well-being and how to build strength into your relationship with good communication skills.

The intention of this book is to address issues that arise in most marriages and convey ideas that have helped other couples. Knowing what to expect when entering marriage can make a critical difference in achieving a satisfying relationship that not only survives, but thrives. It is my hope that the thoughts presented here will serve to stimulate important conversation between two people considering engagement or marriage and result in a decision that will reap the greatest happiness and satisfaction for both individuals. For those of you who are already married, may this book offer some insights to enrich your union.

Introduction

FOR SOME PEOPLE, rhythm comes naturally, while others feel they just cannot dance, period. Some couples dance only when they have no choice, and then, uncomfortably. Accomplished dancers became proficient because they learned the required steps and had a partner who was patient and willing to practice. It is interesting that one of the first things that a couple does after the wedding ceremony is to share their first dance as husband and wife. I believe dancing serves as a perfect metaphor for the marital relationship and serves as the thesis of this book.

Some married couples just seem to bend and weave in unison—they flow. Disruptions seem no more than the occasional misstep. They deal with the issue, move on, seeming not to miss a beat. Then, there is the other extreme with couples who seem to have the constant friction of bumping, sometimes colliding, with each other every step of the way. They just feel clumsy, embarrassed and say, "This is just not for me." They stop dancing. Another group, who may find marriage challenging, is determined to make a go of it. They seek help and try to find out how to do things in another way to make their marriage work. What makes the difference? Like accomplished dancers, they learn some basic steps and then they keep practicing until they get it right. Throughout marriage, a couple has to find its own rhythm, tempo and steps. They need to move with enough smoothness to avoid tripping over each other, thus preventing continual annoyance or even causing harm.

It helps to recognize that marriage, like any relationship, requires give-and-take and good communication. Remember arriving at college and meeting your assigned roommate? Even if you had communicated through social media, you probably never met, yet were expected to live together for an entire semester. Likely, you had to work out a few things.

How about moving into your first apartment with a friend? Even though you knew each other, it was quite different when you had to share the same bathroom and kitchen and maybe had two different work schedules. Just deciding which TV shows to watch, what music to play or how to divide up household chores, took some effort. This holds even more so for marriage because you cannot just ask for a room change or move out without a lot of legal hassle.

Just like dance routines, there are patterns that are formed early in relationships. These dance steps become habits. Communication, for both the routine stuff of everyday life and the emotional stuff of arguments, can set up a dance that is conducive to a loving relationship or steps that are destructive. Some issues can be serious, but, more often, it is a matter of learning to address relatively minor frustrations early on, so that a "tit for tat" dance does not evolve. The marriage may survive, but the dance can leave each partner feeling upset, frustrated and angry. If a healthy pattern is not established, minor things can result in a dance that contaminates what could otherwise be a very loving and satisfying relationship.

Learning to dance together smoothly does not just happen. There will be stepping on toes, twirling the wrong way, gliding independently at times and then, finally, moving in sync to the music. There will be different dances at different stages of your marriage. The dating period is when you can have fun dancing the "Bunny Hop," expending high energy along with some physical contact. Then there is the early dance of marriage when you experience the passion of "The Tango" period. These are often sparse years for many couples with few furnishings, little money and student loans, yet exciting with the anticipation of building a life together.

Taking responsibility for knowing who you are, defining what you want from marriage and what you are willing to give, can help ensure that your relationship is one that will thrive. Learning how to dance together early on can help your marriage flow with less stress and greater happiness. The ability to establish healthy habits will give you the dance steps needed to provide the foundation for staying in sync in the years ahead. No one can predict the future, but the couples who stay on the dance floor are the ones who are there to enjoy "The Waltz" in the later years of their marriage.

What basic dance steps will work best for you? That is for you to learn as a couple. For those of you already married, it is never too late to learn some new moves. The basics of healthy communication, understanding personality differences, dealing with in-laws, achieving sexual compatibility, as well as information on behavioral health, can serve to strengthen any marriage. Learning ways to disagree without being disagreeable, the importance of kindness and the different ways to express love to your mate, can all serve to enrich your union.

There is no greater blessing than a happy marriage, and I wish that for you, no matter what stage you are at in your relationship. So put on your best dancing shoes, grab your partner and head out onto the dance floor.

I

"The Bunny Hop"

THE DANCE OF THE DATING YEARS

"Those marriages generally abound most with love and constancy that are preceded by a long courtship."

—Joseph Addison

"The Bunny Hop"

Some dances make us look or feel silly; some make us happy, others serious, even melancholy. There are some dances where you do not hold your partner and others where you have intimate contact. A couple's dating phase may be compared to an older dance called the "Bunny Hop." This dance originated in 1952 in San Francisco as the "dance party" dance to liven up an occasion. Participants dance in a line, holding on to the hips of the person in front. The dancers tap the floor two times with their right foot and then with their left foot, then they hop forwards, backwards, and finally three hops forward to finish the sequence. As the music speeds up, you can get a serious workout.

Like the Bunny Hop, the dating dance is one that requires practice and energy. But this important time also deserves scrutiny. It is during this dating phase that you should ask "is this the right person for me?" Then, ask the question "is marriage the right choice for me?" These are two life-changing decisions that should never be made in haste. This is a good time for a serious workout, before any commitments or obligations interfere with your better judgment. Make no mistake about it, when you start dating, your dance has begun.

CHAPTER ONE

Knowing Yourself

THERE ARE MANY THINGS that are important to the growth, success, satisfaction and survival of marriage. If I had to choose one, it would be to *know yourself.* Know who you are. Recognize your moods. Know when you feel happy, sad, content, irritable, angry and calm and understand what triggers these emotions. If you can do this, you will gain valuable insight into how to initiate, channel, avoid or control these emotions. Even more importantly, you will be able to communicate this insight to your significant other.

If you do not know who you are, then you are apt to expect your partner to be a mind reader. This is likely to lead to frustration and disappointment when you feel that your spouse fails to meet your expectations. Most married couples would say they are pretty poor mind readers, especially in the early years of the relationship. And the reason is not because your spouse does not care or deliberately wants to annoy you. The real reason is because your spouse does not understand these things about you, yet. Some would say they never get it!

The reason your emotions are unknown to your partner is because he or she is not you. Men and women do not view things the same way. Each of you has your own personality and temperament. Your upbringing, with countless childhood experiences, was different from your partner. Your family's medical and genetic histories are completely distinct. To expect a spouse to understand what you are feeling, without clearly communicating your feelings, is an unrealistic expectation, likely to leave you continually frustrated.

Recognize that you will discover things about your spouse that you will never understand. Stuff that would not even fluff your feathers for a nanosecond may be something that your mate finds really upsetting. I remember a friend's husband who was awful at keeping track of dates, but anniversaries and birthdays were very important to his wife. When he forgot, it would send her into a tailspin of sadness, feeling rejected and unloved. His many other good qualities would seem to evaporate in the wake of one of his memory lapses. With some insight and encouragement, she realized it was better for both of them if she dropped him some reminders a few days ahead of time. He appreciated the hints and she saved herself a lot of misery.

Something that delights your partner may be something you could not care less about. Such things are not on your radar screen, yet they are things that have an emotional effect on your spouse and therefore an impact on your marriage. First day of hunting season may be something you wait for all year. Communicating that to your wife can prevent her from inviting friends over for dinner that weekend. With self insight, you can inform your spouse, with the hope that she will respect your plans for that time.

Sometimes you may find that certain dates or memories of a sad or upsetting event in your life (of which your spouse may not even be aware) trigger a cascade of emotions, from sadness to anger. Subconsciously, this can affect your mood and your attitude toward your spouse, although he or she did nothing to cause it. Inability to recognize this prevents you from talking about the cause of your upset and can be transferred onto an undeserving mate. Instead, if you can each recognize these triggers for yourself, you can share that information, thus allowing for support, rather than resentment, during difficult times.

You each will have your own feelings regarding issues and situations. Those feelings are not right or wrong, good or bad. They are your feelings. They are your partner's feelings. They are personal. The ability for each of you to know yourself and communicate your needs and desires to each other is the epitome of emotional intimacy. It is this willingness to expose your vulnerability that will build the closeness on which a long, loving, and trusting relationship is formed. Take time each day to touch base with each other to share these important insights. This deliberately carved-out period of time can help prevent the recurrence of hurt and resentment. Start now, as it is an ongoing process in your marital dance.

CHAPTER TWO

Packing Your Bag

YOU ARE IN LOVE and considering engagement. Thinking about marriage should be a joyous and exciting feeling. Passion prevails, love has blossomed and your world is a happy place. Everyone should experience this high at least once in their lifetime. As a true romantic, I never tire of hearing about love and romance. Marriage and parenthood, however, are not meant for everyone. This may burst a few bubbles, but in the long run, the choice to forego such decisions may be the right one. Marriage and parenthood are the most life altering and permanent events that any individual will experience in his or her lifetime. Neither the costs nor the rewards of these decisions reflect their true value or the emotions associated with them. Neither vocation is for the faint of heart.

My mother used to say to me, "Susan, if you live long enough, you won't believe what you will see happen in people's lives." The older I get, the more those words rattle in my brain. I just did not realize she was talking about me. My husband and I agree that if our married life had been laid out in front of us before we began our journey, we probably would not have had the courage to get on for the ride. And yet, we also agree we would do it all again. Why? For one, the bad times did not come all at once. Our challenges sometimes presented themselves in bunches, but just when it seemed too much to take, we would have a reprieve. Somehow, given the travails that life presented, love trumped the troubles.

It is encouraging to meet the number of engaged couples who are willing to take on an unknown future with love and abandon. They feel the risk is worth it. Those who take the time to learn what makes for a successful marriage are likely to set their sights more realistically; statistics are on their side for a happy outcome.

I see this dating period as a time to pack your bag with the new dancing shoes that will be worn thin over your years together, as you experience the joys and challenges that await you. Your lessons and the steps you will learn together will help you maneuver life's ups and downs. There are some qualities that seem to be present consistently with long-married couples which contribute to being there for the curtain call. In packing your bag for this exciting trip into the unknown, you might want to reflect on these attributes and talk about how they relate to your life together:

VALUES: A value system is instilled in each of us during our childhood and builds through our formative years. When it comes to melding your life with someone else, there is much less dissention when you share the same moral compass. Couples who share similar values do not have to talk continually about the right choice in a given situation. The role of religion, spending habits, time given to hobbies, career ambitions, the part technology plays in daily life, the decision about whether to live together before marriage, attitude toward elders, children, feelings about pets, and his or her personal habits are some examples that will give insight into your partner's priorities and attitudes. Do you share similar values? If not, can you respect and accept the differences? *Values are unlikely to change.*

FAITH: This is not to be confused with religion, as such, but rather a belief in God or something greater than oneself. Both Patrick and I have strong faith. We have always believed in the saying "God helps those who help themselves." We were brought up to not expect handouts. We anticipated working hard for what we wanted, but many times we had to work a lot harder than we expected. Our faith allowed us to believe the hard work would pay off.

HEALTH: Good health has been a blessing that has allowed Patrick and me the energy to do what needed to be done during the difficult times. We have always taken care of ourselves, but medical issues have arisen nonetheless. Not everyone who takes care of themselves is rewarded with good health. No one can prevent all the possible physical, medical and emotional challenges that life will deal us. Serious health issues can pose one of the biggest challenges to a marriage. How do you and your partner handle the smaller frustrations in life? Is there the ability to make a plan and move forward, or do minor mishaps create such frustration they derail you? Without wanting to dwell on the negative, yet recognizing the inevitability of such events, Patrick reminds couples that marriage will have challenges that you cannot prepare for and that will test your faith, courage and love. Taking responsibility for what you can control: your diet, physical exercise, lifestyle choices and regular medical screenings, can go a long way to ensure the best outcome. It is unfair to expect your spouse to nag you to get regular checkups, seek medical care or counseling, when warranted. Each of you needs to assume responsibility for keeping yourself healthy, physically and emotionally.

PARTNERSHIP: The world is not always a nice place. Bad things do happen to good people and if the foundation of the marriage is built on sand, rather than on cement, it is more likely to be wiped out in the first major storm. Recognizing, early on, the importance of partnership will allow you to set this as a priority that will strengthen your marriage. The greater good of your partnership must reign over individual needs. This concept may be the greatest gift of your marriage and one that is a challenge for some individuals. Building trust, respect, integrity and fidelity into your relationship will give you that solid foundation needed to weather the bigger crises you will face. Patrick has often said that a true partnership provides twice the joy during the happy times and halves the sorrow during the challenges. I agree.

You may find yourself not wanting to bring up topics that could ruin a lovely evening and possibly disrupt this otherwise happy time of your life, but this is the most appropriate time to have such talks. While dating, you do not yet have the pressure of an announced engagement or the financial investment of wedding commitments. You have the delicious freedom to discuss your hopes, dreams, challenges and concerns, and make a private decision as to whether you want to move ahead in your relationship. No one knows what the future holds. Often, it is the very hopes and dreams that you share, not knowing what lies ahead, which keep you together. The good times are easy, but being prepared for the sad, challenging, sometimes heart-wrenching times, is what will test your mettle.

We all bring a certain amount of baggage into our marriage. Early in your relationship is a good time to unpack that suitcase, sort and wash the contents and repack only those items that you want to take on this new journey. Pack your bag with a good pair of dancing shoes and the critical things that have made a positive difference for many couples. It can help ensure that your leap into the unknown will be a loving and rewarding adventure.

CHAPTER THREE

Doing Your Due Diligence

THE WAY MARRIAGE IS PORTRAYED in the media, it would seem that a couple just meets, gets stars in their eyes, falls in love and lives happily ever after. There is little acknowledgment this is one of the most important decisions you will make in your life. There will be few things that will have more effect on your future happiness and well-being. The decision as to whom to marry deserves much scrutiny. Let's just compare it to another decision you will likely make as a young adult: buying your first car.

This is often the first large purchase made as an adult. In making this decision, buyers usually check out a consumer magazine, reviewing different models to familiarize themselves with the pros and cons of each. Next is the decision on what the budget can handle, as far as monthly payments. Test driving follows and, then, the emotional reaction of which one feels right. Once you own the vehicle, it is worth noting how protecting this depreciating investment becomes a priority. Insurance is immediately purchased to cover it for damage, theft and personal liability and some even add coverage for mechanical problems. Next, you sign up for roadside assistance to guard against inconvenience, in case of a dead battery or flat tire. Then, of course, is the all important car mechanic! This is the critical person who knows you and your car and whom you consider to be competent, dependable and honest. The car is inspected, registered and put on the road. Then after 3,000–5,000 miles, the conscientious owner gets the oil changed and fluids checked and makes sure that regular maintenance occurs. Even society has a stake in this with state laws requiring a periodic inspection to confirm that the car is in road-worthy condition and meets environmental standards. Wow, all this for a piece of machinery that, even with the best of care, will eventually go out of style, wear out and fall into disrepair! And the buyer will simply move on to the next car, often with little emotional impact.

When contemplating marriage, can you say that you are giving at least as much time and attention exploring this relationship to ensure the best possible outcome? If such scrutiny is good enough for your car, your life commitment deserves even more. Courtship is the time to do this. Learn about each other's childhood and the influences that made your partner who she/he is. What is important to your potential spouse? What are his aspirations? What are her career plans? Do you both see children as part of your future? What if you cannot have children? Is adoption a consideration? Does your partner value your opinion and insight on different issues? Give yourself the gift of time. Getting to know someone is a process. See and experience each other in many different situations. Do not be afraid to kick the tires. It can help ensure a longer and smoother ride.

CHAPTER FOUR

Assessing Values

IN TALKING WITH LONG MARRIED COUPLES about what they feel is important in a successful relationship, there always seem to be a few words or phrases that tend to be repeated: qualities like "respect," "sense of humor," "patience" and "kindness." But one I hear most consistently stated is "values." One fellow at our 40th college reunion summed it up saying, "A good marriage seems to come down to values. When different issues come up, if you share the same basic values, the decisions are easier to make."

While you are dating, there will be many opportunities to get a sense of your partner's values. During the early stages of any relationship, you can learn a lot if you take note of what you see. Observing how he treats his parents, learning what her childhood was like, noticing how she spends her money, how he manages his, how she reacts to the daily annoyances of life, watching his road manners, how she treats sales people, how he views those less well-off or less educated, what hobbies she has, how he chooses to spend his free time, can all give you insight into what things are important to your potential spouse.

To get a sense of each other's value system and how it relates to your long-term relationship, a professional prenuptial session can be time well spent. This can be done with a pastoral counselor or a non-religious life coach and allows for the opportunity to address various topics. The top four that will inevitably affect the marriage at some point are: money, sex, religion and in-laws.

MONEY: Recognizing the role that money plays in a partnership is as critical to a marriage as it is to a business. Each of us has emotional, as well as practical, experiences with money. It will make a difference if an individual is coming straight from dependency on parents into the marriage or if he or she has lived independently, paying for housing, food, clothing and car costs without having to consult or depend on anyone regarding expenses and how money is spent or saved. Discussion on the type of accounts, who will pay the bills, and spending and saving habits, will be essential to minimize the stress that finances can cause.

We met Alicia and Pete on our honeymoon. We were staying on an island and they were on a cruise. We shared a few fun outings with them before their ship departed. Being the same age, marrying on the same day and enjoying their company, we decided to keep in touch. It was evident from the first honeymoon conversations that Alicia had a target goal to buy a house. It was all she talked about. Every penny was to go into savings for the down payment. Although Pete certainly seemed onboard with the idea, it did not hold the same laser focus for him. He had a hobby of reading and was passionate about purchasing hard cover copies of first edition books. Although this would seem a harmless activity, when related to their marriage, that proved not to be the case.

Because we only lived a couple of hours apart, we were able to have the occasional visit. First, it was our apartment and then theirs. The conversations often focused on the cost of homes, interest rates, equity verses renting. Homeownership made sense to all of us. It was just that no one, especially Pete, was in the same hurry as Alicia. Every time he came home from work with a new book, she went ballistic. That was $25–30 dollars that was not going toward the down payment. Our third visit was to their home, a comfortable ranch style house with a lot of bookshelves! It just never seemed to bring the joy that Alicia expected. The last visit with them was in our first home, shortly after the birth of our first child. After that, it was a Christmas card saying they were divorcing. We do not know all the details, but it is pretty safe to say that finances, spending habits and communications played a role in the breakdown of the marriage. Alicia and Pete seemed to want the same things, but were never able to fully communicate on the strategy or time table for their goals. The dance steps just never got into sequence.

SEX: Sex should be a growing and vibrant part of your marriage. But again, the values statement applies. Be mindful of your partner's attitudes regarding sex. If you have been used to having *Playboy* around your apartment or checking onto porn sites your partner finds offensive, discussion is warranted, with consideration to his or her feelings. Sex should enrich your intimacy, not only the physical aspect, but the emotional and spiritual aspects as well.

Sex will mean different things at different stages of your marriage. Sometimes it will be passionate and fun, while at other times it will be comforting and reassuring. Be cognizant of your partner's mood and needs, and know your own needs. Communicate about what sex means to each of you. Many things go into having a satisfying physical relationship; love and respect are probably among the most important qualities, with open and honest communication being the overarching factor.

To expect a phenomenal sex life in your early marriage is like expecting to sit down for your first piano lesson and playing a concerto. It does not happen like that. It takes time, nurturing, understanding and practice. Even if you have had other relationships, this one is unique. You want this one to be for keeps.

RELIGION: Do you each share the same religion? If not, do you respect the role that religion does, or does not, hold for your partner? Will you be able to support the spiritual beliefs and religious traditions that are important to your spouse? If you have children, can you agree on how the children will be raised? The National Marriage Project based at the University of Virginia linked shared religion with a happy marriage. It supports the old aphorism, "couples who pray together, stay together."

Patrick and I both felt attending church weekly was important to us, so this was not an issue that required deliberation every weekend. He tells the engaged couples that there has been many a Sunday when we were headed to church and he was so angry with me that he did not want to sit next to me. The children were often a natural buffer and we could sandwich the four of them between us in the long wooden pew, looking for all the world like the perfect, happy family. Then, the readings and the homily came, which he says always had a message he felt was directed at him. The "Our Father" followed, during which we were supposed to hold hands, and then the dreaded "Kiss of Peace!" Patrick says, "you would not believe how lightly you can brush a cheek when you are angry. But you have to do it because the kids are waiting and everybody is looking. Then she squeezes my hand and I smile, even when I don't want to, but it's over. Not being there would have allowed the argument to fester for the entire day and maybe beyond," he concludes. And I can ditto that. There is a good chance you will hear a message in a house of worship that will not be found in the four walls at home. I reflect on my classmate's previous statement on values; if there are similar attitudes about the importance of religion in your life, then you will figure out how to incorporate the role of worship into your marriage.

IN-LAWS: What expectations does your partner's family

have regarding traditions and celebrations? If your mate is from a different culture, with traditions unlike the ones you were raised with, can you accept them as part of your married life? Are you both independent from the financial support of your parents? Taking on fiscal responsibility is the first step in establishing your autonomy. You are then in a position of equal footing to talk with your parents about the decisions and choices you are making and less beholding to their opinions.

No marriages have the perfect match when it comes to these issues. And of course, there will be the unexpected events life will inevitably present. Having a similar value system will make it less likely that such challenges will derail your marriage. Do not be afraid of differences, they can enrich your relationship and family. With no credit to us, Patrick and I have much in common: we met in college, we are the same age (though he will always be older!), and we share the same religion, have the same friends, our parents had intact marriages, we share similar political views and we are both extroverts. It would be deceptive of me not to admit this serendipity of characteristics has allowed for less discord. This is not the case for most couples. Differences need not be a deterrent to a rewarding marriage, but they do need to be acknowledged. Although the saying is "opposites attract," there is less friction when couples have more qualities in common.

It is the wise couple who can recognize differences and embrace them for the richness they can bring to a marriage. There are things you can live with, and things you can compromise on. There may also be things that are in opposition to your core values: dishonesty, meanness, selfishness, intolerance, jealousy, lack of integrity, love of money, substance misuse. Such things may be deal breakers. And it is good to realize those before becoming engaged.

CHAPTER FIVE

Liking Your Spouse

DURING AN INTERVIEW with a long married couple, the wife commented to the reporter that as angry as she may get at her husband at times, she still really liked him. There is a lot of importance in that simple, but very powerful statement, for it holds the truth as to what is critical to a healthy and thriving marriage.

The aggravations of daily life are many, especially during the career building and child rearing years. The idiosyncrasies of your spouse can grate on each of you over time. Frustrations over the way certain situations are handled can cause real eruptions. The long hours your spouse is spending at work or the discipline that is meted out for a child's infraction can cause many heated discussions. There are times you do not want to be in the same room with your spouse. The picture of marital bliss can be very hard to recognize at such moments.

During these times, it is easy to want to throw in the towel. Leave. It could be easy to do, if you did not like the person. The respect you have for your spouse, the values and integrity displayed in daily life can serve to bring perspective to the situation. Sometimes there will be no real agreement on an issue, but a respect for your partner's opinion in a given situation can make it easier to accept the differences and talk about compromise.

It is the wise person who, at some point in the early part of a relationship (and sooner would be better than later), can put passion on the shelf for a moment and ask "do I like this person? Do I enjoy his personality and her sense of humor? When the passion wanes and life becomes more mundane, when the tango morphs into line dancing, will I be happy to wake up in morning with this person beside me? Do I respect who he or she is and how they behave, not only with me, but with others?" These can be tough questions to ask when we just want to be happy and not look at some of the deeper issues. Asking these questions now can save disappointment and emotional pain down the road for both of you.

Most of your married life is going to be spent interacting and dealing with other people in work, community, social and family situations. Character flaws are not to be ignored during this time of courtship, as there will be even less time later on to explore these questions thoughtfully. Rest assured, in the years ahead, those things you do not admire, respect or enjoy about your partner are likely to be ongoing sources of irritation, embarrassment and conflict in your marriage. When the hormones have cooled, you want to like the partner you chose. Having a deep and enduring friendship, is one of the greatest assets to a happy and healthy marriage.

CHAPTER SIX

Noting Personality Differences

DO YOU EVER WONDER WHY your spouse reacts a certain way, when your inclination is entirely the opposite? One of the early encounters during our college dating days first brought home the point we would not always be on the same page. We had planned to meet outside the cafeteria at 6:00 p.m. and have dinner together. I was feeling all warm and fuzzy about seeing Patrick and not the least concerned that I was running late. How was I to know he was tired and starving and with every minute his annoyance was growing? By the time I bounced in, with the then popular song, *Little Green Apples* playing in my head, thinking he would be oh so happy to see me, his face showed he was less than enthralled.

Personality types were first described by the Greek physician, Hippocrates, about 2400 years ago. Throughout the years, social scientists have written extensively, describing various combinations of temperamental traits. Different authors write about combinations of characteristics, identifying as many as sixteen personality types. In her book *Personality Plus,* Florence Littauer talks about four basic personality styles. Although we possess qualities of each of them, there is one personality type that is dominant in each of us. The names assigned to the four basic types often vary, depending on the source, but the descriptions are similar.

Brief descriptions of the four basic types are:

- ◆ THE SANGUINE (THE EXPRESSIVE): This temperament is fundamentally an extrovert, impulsive and fun

27

loving. They are very social, make new friends easily and tend to be boisterous, but they also can be sensitive, thoughtful and compassionate. "Expressives" tend to be chronically late, can be forgetful and do not always follow through on tasks. This personality type will often be the one who finishes your sentences or gives your punch line! They do not lack confidence.

♦ THE CHOLERIC (THE DRIVER): This temperament is ambitious and displays leadership qualities. They have a take-charge kind of personality which can be intimidating to others. Political and military leaders tend to fall into this category. Interestingly, they can be either very organized or disorganized and those extremes can carry over to having mood swings.

♦ THE PHLEGMATIC (THE AMIABLE): This temperament tends to be relaxed, quiet and more of a watcher, than a doer or initiator. They tend to be kind and content with themselves and may seem lazy at times. They tend to resist change and prefer family stability. Because they usually are calm, rational and observant, they tend to be good administrators. They are often known to be passive-aggressive, a characteristic that can make them challenging at times. They can be the easiest personality type to be around because they tend to agree with the prevailing opinions, yet frustrating when they seem to not take a stand on an issue.

♦ THE MELANCHOLY (THE ANALYTICAL): This temperament is more introverted and thoughtful. They are considerate and can be very creative. They can worry about being late and tend to project that worry to include the disruption in the world. They are often perfectionists who tend to be self-reliant and independent. Because they can focus on a task, they can forget to consider others. They are thinkers, organized and like to be right.

So you can see there are strengths and weaknesses in each type and one is not better than another. When taken to an extreme, the dominant trait can cause problems for an individual and his or her relationships. When the Sanguine/ Expressive type is excited about going to the new movie in town and spontaneously greets the Melancholy/Analytical spouse with the prospect of going that evening, there may be a response like, "what, tonight?" Followed by, "I haven't read the movie reviews yet, and actually, I thought I would organize my tool bench tonight."

There are personality inventories to determine which type is dominant. Myers-Briggs Personality Test© and PeopleMap™ Personality Assessment are two popular ones. This information can be helpful in understanding your own and your partner's personality traits and how they affect your behaviors. And if you do not know which one you are most like, just ask your partner. Chances are he or she has a pretty good idea!

We know couples where the wives are very outgoing, engaging and chatty. The husbands can spend an entire evening, seeming perfectly content, and not utter a single word in group conversation. Such is the life of extrovert married to an introvert. They accept and enjoy their spouse and recognize that they are not going to change their innate personality. They have long-term happy marriages with a dance routine that suits both of them.

None of these traits needs to be a deal breaker in a marriage. Awareness of the characteristics of the different personality and temperament types can allow you to play to each other's strengths while minimizing the weaknesses. When you come to understand certain traits in your spouse, you will better know how to approach topics and how to make plans, with some effort to avoid repeated conflict. One couple I know who have been married many years may come to an event at separate times to preserve his need for being punctual and hers for being more casual about time. This may require changing the dance routine on a regular basis over the course of your relationship, but think of all the exercise you will get!

CHAPTER SEVEN

"Cluttering Up Your Closet"

"MAKE SURE YOU LOVE YOUR PURCHASE, because you will never like it better than you do in the store." That was the advice from a retail fashion diva regarding clothes shopping. I never thought of a purchase like that before, but it makes such sense. "You want to be really excited about owning this piece of your wardrobe," she said, "because as soon as you get home, it will become just another thing hanging in your closet."

A few days after hearing that, my niece called and was relating her weekend at a bachelorette party of a close college friend. My niece had flown from Chicago to Fort Lauderdale to meet with five girlfriends and have a fun girls' weekend celebrating the upcoming wedding. I shared my "oh, what fun" reaction followed by "did you have a great time?" To which she responded flatly, "no, not really." What?

They all arrived late on Friday evening at different times, so they decided to stay in the hotel room and have pizza and relax. That evening, she reported, the bride got "totally wasted." The next evening they did the town, hitting all the local bars with the bride-to-be decked out in the little white veil with her bridal party in tow. She said the girl was sullen most of the evening and, again, drank too much. I asked what the problem was. My niece went on to say that none of the friends liked her fiancé and they do not even bring up his name anymore. When asked if anyone had spoken to her about whether or not she wanted to get married, she assured me it had been brought up a number of times and the bride's response was a rather unemotional, "Well, we have been together for six years. It's about time, don't you think?" Of course with the wedding two weeks away, everything had been finalized and paid for, just adding to the stress. But the words of the retail diva just rang in my head. Wow, if she is not over the moon about him now, what is it going to be like in three months, three years; just another person with clothes cluttering up the closet?

In these weeks before your wedding, should you not be supremely happy at the thought of your marriage and the excitement of spending the rest of your life with this person? This is supposed to be the time of the ultimate anticipation and wanting to share this joy with your friends and family. Even with the stress of wedding preparations, the exhilaration of the end result should trump that stress.

While appreciating the difficulty of the situation, both emotionally and financially, I encouraged my niece to have someone talk to her and offer to go with her to meet with her parents and discuss her concerns now. Even with the embarrassment and the inevitable cost, it will certainly be a lot less costly, emotionally and financially, then dealing with the heartache waiting down the road.

I later learned from my niece, that her friend did call off her wedding, four days before the ceremony. She apparently was driving home from work after not having seen her fiancé for several days and realized that she was not looking forward to seeing him. Dreading going home before you are even married??? Then it hit her, that if this is how she felt now, what would it be like for the rest of their lives? Yes, family and friends had already flown in and money was lost, but a lot of heartache and more expense down the road were spared for everyone.

So this girl mustered up the courage to make a painful decision and that was a good thing. But how much less painful it would have been if the relationship had ended before things had become so complicated. Nobody's marriage is perfect. You will not find everything you want in your spouse, nor will you be the perfect partner. Recognizing early on what is important to you in your relationship gives you a chance to decide what you can accept and live with and what you cannot. Knowing the difference greatly increases the odds of your long-term happiness.

CHAPTER EIGHT

Feeling the Magic

DO YOU REMEMBER the 1993 movie *Sleepless in Seattle* with Meg Ryan and Tom Hanks? In one scene, Meg's character, Annie, stops in at her parents' home with her fiancé, Walter. She is in the attic trying on her mother's wedding gown, when her mother, misty eyed, comments, "it's just magic, isn't it?" Annie looks quizzically at her mother, "Magic?" She really has no idea what her mother means. Certainly Annie cares about Walter. She may even love him, but it was very evident from her response and reaction that she was not "in love" with him and felt no magic at all.

The word "magic" is not meant in a frivolous way. It goes beyond physical attraction. While there are many ingredients critical to long lasting love that are important, a sense of magic adds a dimension that cannot be measured. It is that tingle of anticipation you feel when you know you are going to see each other. It is that feeling that seems to make everyone else in the room fade into the background.

Now scientists have found a physiologic basis for the sensation those in love feel. In her 2004 book, *Why We Love— The Nature and Chemistry of Romantic Love*, Helen Fisher writes about the chemical reaction that has been documented by magnetic resonance imaging (MRI). It shows the interaction of hormones and neurotransmitters that create the sensation those in love have experienced. Dopamine, norepinephrine, oxytocin and serotonin are the key players that dictate such feelings. They are responsible for the butterflies, the excitement of being in love, the calmness that takes over after the initial anxiety of new love, the hope that the other cares as much as you do and, finally, the trust and bond that connects the two of you.

"Magic" cannot be the only ingredient if a relationship is to last a lifetime. But when difficult times hit, or even simple annoyances occur, it is often the salve that makes a difference. "Magic" can allow you to remember the qualities that attracted you in the first place and the ones you have come to respect and admire in your mate. And that "magic," for those who know it, can be the very thing that carries you through to "The Waltz."

CHAPTER NINE

Meeting the Family

PATRICK FIRST MET MY PARENTS when he dropped me off from college for Thanksgiving break. We were not yet officially dating. He recalls how my mother announced that my fifteen year old brother had run away after another adolescent confrontation, and my father was about ready to kill him. Then, my Dad thanked Patrick for bringing me home, as he informed me that my boyfriend had called. It was a memorable first meeting!

I was first introduced to my future in-laws on Christmas Eve. I arrived at Patrick's home where I met his Mom, a lively, attractive woman whose opinionated manner was softened by a charming, Irish brogue. Years later, she could name every article of clothing, even the colors, that I wore that evening. The night she met me, she later told me, she knew instantly that I was the girl for her son. Patrick's Dad greeted me like we had met before. I felt the same. He strode across the room with the warmth of a charming leprechaun and grasped my frosty hand with both his warm ones and placed a kiss on my chilly cheek. If I had any doubts about his son, I knew immediately that I wanted him for my father-in-law! And for the next twenty-one years until his death, there was never a day I felt differently.

* * *

When dating becomes serious, couples usually are interested in meeting their partner's family. Sometimes one or both may not be as excited to introduce this special person, whom they are considering marrying, to parents and siblings. They may be worried about what impression will be made, or what embarrassing stories may be shared.

Seeing the future spouse in the context of the family is important. Watching the dynamic between the Mom and Dad can shed light on the modeling that likely shaped the perception of the marital relationship. Observe how they talk to each other. What is the tone of voice? Are basic manners practiced? How do they show courtesy and respect for one another? If the parents are divorced, have they managed a civil relationship?

Patrick's parents had a smooth and compatible dance and were both funny and respectful with each other. His Mom's occasional nagging was taken in stride, a further credit to his Dad's good nature. My parents did not have the same levity as Patrick's parents. They had a different dance. It was a dance they made work for their marriage, but they had to work harder at it, having quite different temperaments. We have always felt blessed that our parents demonstrated dedication to their marriage and responsibility in raising their families. They both provided examples we came to appreciate and respect as we created our own dance, discarding some steps and adding others.

Remember, for better or worse, your major role model for marriage is that of your parents. What aspects of your parents' marriage do you admire and respect? If it is a marriage that you do not want to emulate, then talk about how you would like things to be different. What habits do you find concerning? The behavior each of you displays, and the expectations you hold for your marriage, will certainly have a profound effect on the long-term outcome. Do not leave this discussion to chance. It will help you define what you want for yourselves.

The place in the family and the relationship your partner has with siblings and parents can tell you a lot about his or her needs. It can give insight about the expectations for future in-law gatherings. With divorced parents there can be two sets of in-laws, as well as step siblings to consider. Will there be a social connection or will holidays be the extent of it? Are there traditional expectations, like weekly dinners at the in-laws that are part of the package? How does your potential spouse feel about set obligations? Is there flexibility and openness in dealing with such family situations? Is it expected that you will live in the hometown?

Having many opportunities to observe each other within the context of the family will allow you to assess the impact these relationships will have on your marriage. Observe how your partner interacts with his or her parents. Is the manner considerate, respectful? There is an old adage that advises to watch how a man treats his mother, for he will treat his wife the same. Certainly, the behavior that a woman tolerates during the courtship and marriage will affect whether this axiom becomes a reality, but it is worth noting. Letting your own expectations be known can certainly help define your relationship.

Discussions can be very valuable, and you should remember, although you are not responsible for the family you were born into, you are now each responsible for the family that you want to create. As overwhelming as that may seem, it is also very exciting to know you do not have to repeat the past, but rather are free to define your expectations for your future family and create your own dance.

CHAPTER TEN

Communicating

PATRICK SHARES THIS STORY with the engaged couples about one of the "discussions" we had early in our marriage. "I was stretched out in the recliner, eyes closed, with both arms behind my head, as Susan talked about something that I had likely screwed up! When she accused me of not listening, I responded 'I am too listening.' I then parroted back everything she had said. Then she came back with, 'but you are not even looking at me.' I realized she was right. Having eye contact is basic to effective communication. I was young and stupid and I was behaving rudely." All the men in the group give a chuckling groan.

Patrick was not the only person who encountered difficulties in the communication arena. After numerous missteps, we tried to learn from our mistakes. Timing has been one of the many challenges. I found that I would like to fix things NOW. Let's hash it out and talk it through and be done with it. That approach did not work very well. A cooling off period seemed to work better. The caution was remembering to get back to the issue at hand, so it did not get swept under the rug. Such an approach can leave bumps that will likely trip up your dance at a later time. Set a time when things have calmed down, to talk about the issue.

There are several fundamental steps to enhance communication in many areas of your life, not the least of which is your marriage. These are easy to learn, but hard to implement in the heat of an argument. You may have grown up in a home where you did not witness healthy communication. The good news is effective communication is a learned behavior, so it can be re-learned. Like any skill, the more you practice, the better you will become. Some steps to consider:

1. Set a time for discussion, not likely to be interrupted.
2. Shut off all technology.
3. Have direct eye contact.
4. Learn to talk in the first person, "I." (The minute anyone points at us and says "you," in a stressed tone of voice, the less we hear. We are too busy feeling defensive and gearing up for the rebuttal.)
5. Talk about what happened from your perspective. "I did not hear from you that you were running late."
6. Talk about how it made you feel. "I was worried about you and then felt angry when I had dinner waiting and I didn't know where you were."
7. Then (my favorite!) "Next time:" "I know you have to run late sometimes, but *next time*, if you could just give me a call, then I wouldn't worry and I can hold off dinner." (This phrase gives hope that this will not be a recurring issue.) How can you both handle a situation differently in the future?
8. Listen to your partner's perspective and do not be shocked that it may be totally different than yours. Hence, the need for respect and compromise.

These same techniques can be used with co-workers or friends, as they are non-accusatory and direct. Women are often accused of wanting to "talk things to death." Men are often accused of "stonewalling." Noted psychologist and relationship expert Dr. John Gottman defines it as the refusal to discuss an issue and refers to in his book, *The Seven Principles for Making Marriage Work*. A technique that allows for compromise on these two extremes that has helped couples is:

1) define the problem once; 2) focus on solutions. This way your discussions are more succinct and can shed more light than heat. Possibilities present themselves without continual blaming.

Not all issues in your marriage will be easily resolved, but knowing the essentials of healthy and effective communication should lessen some of the inevitable frustrations that occur in every marriage. For more in-depth skills at couple communication, Harville Hendrix, Ph.D. shares the techniques of Mirroring, Validating and Empathizing in his book *Getting the Love You Want*. Reflecting to your spouse what you think you heard and respecting the feelings expressed, even when you may not understand them, are skills that can be practiced and learned. Taking advantage of such professional resources increases your dancing skills and makes it less likely you will continually be stepping on each other's toes.

CHAPTER ELEVEN

Deciding on Sex

FOR DECADES as a pediatric nurse practitioner, I have worked with new parents and their infants and have witnessed a spectrum of situations. There have been many happily married couples who excitedly anticipated the birth of their baby and welcomed him into a loving household. I also have worked extensively with adolescent moms, some of whom were not sure of the father's last name, did not know where he worked or had no information on paternal health history. Some single fathers have stayed involved and accepted their responsibility. Too many men have neglected their role. In these latter situations one might ask, why would a woman have sex with someone she knew so little about? Why would a man father a child and then abdicate all responsibility? Those are fair and good questions and ones I have faced repeatedly over the years.

The explanations vary, but point out the important and powerful role that sex plays in our lives as human beings. The variety of reasons have included: impulsiveness with no thought to prevention ("it just happened / we didn't really think about it"); disruptive family situations; influence of substances; poverty; lack of education; cognitive limitations; history of physical, emotional or sexual abuse from childhood that has not been acknowledged, addressed or adequately treated. Sometimes there is the need to feel loved, not only during the act, but also to have a baby, as someone who will love them back. Obviously, none of these are healthy reasons for having intercourse or becoming pregnant.

Before engagement is a good time to talk about everything and sex is certainly one of those topics. Sexual intimacy adds another dimension to a relationship and, if one is not ready, it can complicate things. It is a good reason to delay intimacy until you have covered some ground and are committed to the relationship. Intercourse is not something that should just happen one night, with regrets afterward. It adds a new layer of concern and risk that is best delayed until you know you are ready for commitment and can fully accept the responsibilities that go along with a possible pregnancy. Are you physically, financially, emotionally, spiritually and legally ready to meet the needs of a baby, should a pregnancy occur? My job as a nurse practitioner continually reminded me how important these questions are for the well being of the baby, as well as the parents. Unfortunately, these have often not been discussed, or even thought about earlier.

To look at media today, one can surmise that admitting one is a virgin is viewed as more an embarrassment than admitting to having had several sexual partners. The humor in the 2005 movie, *The 40-Year-Old Virgin* certainly demonstrates that this mantra is not something to be proud of, but rather to be "fixed" as soon as possible. Women are often portrayed as abnormal if they are not engaging in sex after a few dates, especially if money has been spent on some nice evenings. To view current sit-coms, advertisements and movies, the unmistakable message is everyone is having sex often and with anyone and, if you are not, then you are a prude or something is wrong with you. Sex sells. It just does not always leave a person as satisfied and fulfilled, as the media would have you believe. Rarely, if ever, do the media show the negative side effects of intercourse. The emotional havoc of unplanned sex, such as sexually transmitted diseases, unwanted pregnancy or broken relationships are rarely portrayed. (That would educate, not entertain.)

If a concern over possible sexual incompatibility arises, you might want to ask, "Is this an audition? Who am I being compared to?" To expect to be perfectly matched in the early period of a relationship and be attuned to each other's needs is like expecting to be proficient at a sport that you have never played. Like any skill, a satisfying physical relationship takes practice. Being sexually compatible is not something you are, it is something you become. (Notice how the non-dancer participants in *Dancing with the Stars* become proficient with practice? It is hard to believe they were not accomplished dancers at the beginning!) When the emotional needs of each partner are met, there are rarely sexual problems that cannot be fixed. A satisfying sexual relationship is much more likely to happen over time in a secure and loving marriage. Ongoing tuning and communication will be essential to keeping it vibrant and rewarding.

In his book *Passionate Marriage*, Dr. David Schnarch, bases much of his writing on his theory of "differentiation." He states that "partners who aren't dependent on each other's validation to feel okay about themselves fuel their marriage with their unique strengths, rather than their mutual weaknesses." The time of dating is an ideal time for each partner to fortify his or her self confidence and a sense of independence. Knowing who you are as an individual, what you believe in and what your needs are, can only make your partnership a far stronger union emotionally and, ultimately, physically as well.

Along with a high percentages of couples living together before marriage, there is an increasing number of educated thirty-something year old women who are choosing to have a baby, regardless of marriage. This is a paradigm shift in our culture and does not have to portend a negative outcome.

Many of these couples decide on marriage at a later time. The important elements are the commitment to each other, and the responsibility for caring for the child.

It is important that you both assess your readiness and know how committed you are to this relationship before engaging in sex. This should be a decision that each of you makes willingly and confidently. For those who have chosen to wait until the commitment of marriage, there never seems to be the issue of regret. That can only serve to strengthen your relationship over the years ahead. Learning these basic dance steps together can lead you to becoming great ballroom dancers.

CHAPTER TWELVE

Sliding or Deciding

WOULD IT BE BETTER to know ahead of time that living separately would actually increase your chances of having a successful marriage? The decision to move in with each other may seem simple; "Let's see if we like living together before we go to the expense of a wedding and the commitment of marriage." If couples who cohabitate do not break up within two years, they usually end up getting married. That statistic, from a 2002 study of federal data, indicates that couples do not look at living together as the long-term plan. They generally see it as an arrangement that will either end with a break-up or marriage. What is most interesting is that rather than ensuring greater success for their marriage, couples who cohabitate are often among the highest risk for divorce. Pregnant nineteen-year olds hold the number one slot, while second marriages are number two and couples who cohabitate are the third highest for divorce. You might think that they knew what they were getting into, so there should be fewer surprises. Unfortunately, that is generally not the case. There are some factors, however, that do affect that outcome.

The 2002 report from the National Center for Health Statistics was based on a National Survey of Family Growth, with a sample of almost 13,000 men and women ages 15–44. It found that in an era when about two-thirds of couples who marry live together first, a different picture is emerging, in which there are few differences between those who cohabit and those who do not. In the conflicting studies that come out of research from various universities, one factor that seems significant is how and when the decision is made to move in together.

Those couples who admit "it just happened," seem to be at the highest risk. Researchers have labeled the situation as "sliding, not deciding." Those couples who seriously intend to marry, or are formally engaged, seem to fare better in the ten year studies. At the Center for Marital and Family Studies at the University of Denver, Drs. Scott M. Stanley, Galena Kline Rhoades and Howard J. Markman found "the nature of commitment at the time of cohabitation is what's important." The study was published September 7, 2006 titled "Sliding Versus Deciding: Inertia and the Premarital Cohabitation Effect." The commitment, rather than the "try it out" attitude, would appear to increase the likelihood for long-term success.

Lots of reasons are cited for making the decision to move in together; "We'll save money," "everyone else is doing it," and "let's see if we are compatible" are among the most common. The first two are easy enough to understand, but they do not make a strong argument. The "we'll save money" does not stand up because if you each lived with a roommate you would still be paying half the expenses. The "everyone else is" is right up there with what your mother would say; "if everyone else jumped off the bridge would you do it to?" The third one is the most interesting. What is it about 'compatibility?' Do you want to know if he leaves his pajamas on the floor? Does she squeeze the toothpaste from the middle? Are these really going to be deal breakers? Is there a concern regarding sexual compatibility? Exactly what role does kindness, communication and time, not to ignore love, play in attaining a satisfying sex life?

Couples who lived together are generally less satisfied with marriage after the honeymoon than those who did not live together. In an April 15, 2012 New York Times article

"The Downside of Cohabiting before Marriage" researchers stated that both men and women agreed that their standards for a live-in partner are lower than they are for a spouse. Even though the National Marriage Project from 2001 (then at Rutgers, now at the University of Virginia) found that close to two-thirds of couples believed that living together before marriage was a good way to avoid divorce, their experience has contradicted that belief. Is it perhaps that couples who cohabitate take more freedoms in their daily lives because they are not married yet? Then after the wedding, do they expect their spouse to behave differently and feel resentful when nothing has changed? "I always played pick-up basketball on Monday and Wednesday night, you knew that" he states exasperatedly or she moans, "you know that Thursdays were always the girls' movie night." Old habits are not so easily broken. When everything is the same as before, does disenchantment set in? If not soon weeded out, those habits can take a dangerous choke-hold on the relationship.

One couple we knew, who were older when they got married, wisely recognized that having lived on their own for several years, they had each established their own routines and that married life was going to be very different for each of them. They mutually agreed to put former involvements on hold for a while, as they established their routines as a couple. Eventually they carved out their individual spaces again, but always respecting their marriage first and foremost.

Research also shows that the longer a couple has lived together, the more likely they are to break up. That seems counterintuitive. But is there resentment, sometimes with both individuals, that they were living like they were married and should have enjoyed those "single" years more, instead of "settling in" too soon? Do they then want more freedom, thinking it would be more fun? Meg Jay, Ph.D., a clinical psychologist, and author of *The Defining Decade: Why Your*

Twenties Matter and How to Make the Most of Them Now, states in an article (New York Times, April 15, 2012) that "far from safeguarding against divorce and unhappiness, moving in with someone increases the chance of a mistake or of spending too much time on a mistake." She further quoted a mentor of hers as saying, "the best time to work on someone's marriage, is before he or she has one. And in our era, that may mean before cohabitation." Prevention is always easier than trying to fix things after the fact.

It is important to realize that many couples who live together before marriage often feel the unstated reason—fear of commitment. This fear may come from witnessing their parents' unhappy marriage, experiencing parental divorce, or lacking the confidence or the economic means of living on their own. Are you afraid of failure and want to try it out first by living together? Taking more time to date, getting to know each other and explore contentious topics without the pressures of living together can add another dimension to your relationship. Dr. Scott Stanley, P. E. Amato, Howard Markham from the University of Denver found in their 2006 study that premarital education reduces the divorce rates for participants by thirty percent. This gives couples the opportunity to uncover areas of concern and address them before moving in together.

When each partner can look at the other and say without any doubt, "I can make it on my own. I can take care of myself physically, emotionally and spiritually and support myself financially, but I want to spend my life with you," there will never be any question about the motivation to marry. Is that not the way that each of us wants to be chosen?

CHAPTER THIRTEEN

Recognizing High Maintenance

WHEN WE WERE IN COLLEGE, Patrick had a 1964 Rambler. He frustratingly referred to it as "The Ramblin' Wreck." When he went out to start it, he would carry the keys in one hand and the jumper cables in the other. When those minus-ten degree temperatures arrived in New Hampshire, even the jumper cables were not enough. The "Ramblin' Wreck" was definitely a "high maintenance vehicle." It was just not predictable. But since it was his only means of transportation, he had no choice but to "make do" until he could afford a more dependable car.

Do you know any high maintenance people? You know, the ones who need to be "jump started" every time you see them. Things are never quite right with them. Something always seems to need fixing. These people often have endearing and redeeming qualities. They have to; otherwise no one would keep their company. They can be very loyal friends, compassionate and caring, but, boy, can they be tiring! They are often unable to find a sense of peace for themselves. Rather, they rely on others to pump them up. That can work for a while. You pump them up, only to find that with the next slight downturn, they are deflated again. If he or she is your friend, you have the option to take them in small doses, so as not to exhaust your better nature. If he or she is your potential spouse, however, be forewarned.

Remember the high maintenance car that we could not wait to unload? As soon as we could afford some new wheels, we traded it in and got something more dependable. The time and energy it freed up, to say nothing of the money saved in repair bills, was energizing. But trading in a car is one thing. Getting rid of a spouse is something else. See how she behaves under the adverse situations of everyday life. Check his attitude and resilience when a storm blows through and dampens those spark plugs. Can she take responsibility for her own moods and circumstances without having to rely on you for a tune up all the time? A high maintenance car may be a mechanic's delight, but it is not for everybody. Be aware, be alert and kick the tires. Decide what you can live with and choose wisely. Happy motoring predicts a much smoother dance.

CHAPTER FOURTEEN

Reflecting on the Family of Origin

I ONCE READ A LETTER TO "DEAR ABBY" in which a woman wrote that she was concerned that she would not be a good wife for the man she was seriously dating. She loved him very much and respected his fine qualities, but stated that her parents' marriage had been loveless. She felt that her mother had not been emotionally caring toward her father. Because of her fear at repeating such behavior, she was considering ending the relationship, to spare her partner a lifetime of misery. Her mature insight could actually bode well for a healthy, strong marriage.

There is no denying it; our family has a profound impact on our life. Biologically, our family determines our DNA and genetic make-up. The color of our eyes, quirks of our personality and aspects of our temperament can be traced to some family members we may have never even met. I should have realized this when I gave birth to two redheaded babies. Patrick, as a black haired father, and I, a brunette mother, could only question, "Wherever did these two come from?" It did not take long before my in-laws informed us how many of their siblings had red hair. Perhaps we should have wondered then what other traits may have been passed on!

Environmentally, the family provides the experiences and situations to which we are exposed. Some children are fortunate to be born and raised in families where they are valued and loved. The discipline is firm, fair and consistent. Others are raised in households where they experience behavior that is anything but loving: physical, emotional or sexual abuse, alcoholism, drug use or domestic violence between their parents. These are behaviors that have a negative impact on the physical and psychological development of a child, whether they are a victim or a witness to it. Such experiences are ones that a person would like to forget, or at least deny and certainly not discuss. To do so is simply burying emotions which can become serious baggage when one is working to establish a mature and loving adult relationship.

Whatever the case, it is wise to accept the reality of your family of origin and that of your spouse-to-be. You cannot choose your inherited characteristics, or the family in which you were raised. What really matters, is how you play the hand you are dealt. Are you willing to seek counseling to address these issues, with the hope of lessening the negative impact on your marriage? That is the responsibility you have to yourself and your partner, if you want to move toward a long-term, healthy, thriving and emotionally satisfying relationship.

CHAPTER FIFTEEN

Fighting Fairly

THE DATING PERIOD IS A GOOD TIME to learn how you each handle difficult issues. Recognize your reactions when arguments are escalating. Can you disagree without being disrespectful? Can you argue while avoiding destructive words and actions? Can you be articulate enough to avoid profanity? Hurtful words can leave long-lasting emotional scars.

When asked "what are the three most important words in a relationship," many people might respond, "I love you." I disagree. I believe they are, "I am sorry." Many of us find those words difficult to say. One way to prevent having to apologize is to avoid saying what you are thinking and feeling at the time of an argument, when you are the angriest. Going for a walk or run, heading to the gym, pounding a pillow or writing madly in your journal may help relieve the initial physical and emotional tension. Giving each other space and a cooling off period can allow for a more productive and healthier discussion later.

One mistake many couples make is that they just move on, thinking the issue has passed, only to find that it resurfaces later when they are arguing about an unrelated topic and the old one raises its ugly head. Arguing about money one evening and one of you yells, "Your mother was positively rude last week and you didn't even stick up for me." This is how unresolved issues can snowball onto each other, making it more difficult to sort out how to address them.

Men are often accused of wanting to drop the issue. Women are often accused of talking it to death. There is a balance between these two extremes and I think it may be one of the more important dances that you learn in your married life. Discovering the steps that work best for you can prevent you from repeating a pattern that brings little resolution to the situation. The important thing is to reconnect when things are calmer and you have had a chance to mentally process the problem. Stating your feelings in a non-accusatory way makes it much more likely that you will each feel you are being heard.

Dr. John Gottman states that some issues in your relationship will never be resolved. This does not mean these issues have to be deal breakers for your marriage. They should, however, be listened to and respectfully acknowledged by each partner. In his book, *Why Marriages Succeed or Fail*, Dr. Gottman notes that it is not the differences between a couple, but rather *how* they address their differences that will determine the satisfaction and outcome of a marriage. Do not be afraid of arguments. They provide the opportunity for a couple to share their opinions and passion which can, when handled with respect, result in greater intimacy in your relationship.

We all know couples who have a solid marriage who deal with issues in totally different ways. Some couples are very emotional in their disagreements, with a lot of yelling and door slamming. This style would overwhelm those individuals who tend to go to great lengths to avoid such outbursts. As a result, they seem to avoid confronting their differences. Other couples seem to fall somewhere in the middle, tending to address their issues in a calmer manner, trying to work out their problems together. The good news is that Dr. Gottman's research shows that all three styles can experience long term, satisfying marriages. Again, the difference seems to be finding a balance, the right dance that works for both of you. Without the right steps, you can find yourselves continually arguing about the same issues, leaving each of you feeling chronically frustrated and unhappy.

Learning the techniques for a smoother dance is possible. Knowledge is power. Like any skill you want to improve upon, read what the experts say, and share what you learn with each other. Practice some new approaches. If it does not seem to lead to improvement, seek out individual and couple counseling. Remember the early metaphor about the investment you are willing to make in your car? You may tinker with minor mechanical problems yourself, but if your car continues to skip, you will seek out your trusted car mechanic to get you back on the road. Does your marriage deserve any less?

CHAPTER SIXTEEN

Addressing Behavioral Health

I REMEMBER ATTENDING a church wedding several years ago. An elegant reception followed, after which we went to the home of the bride's parents. Shortly thereafter, the bride and groom showed up. They had already bought a home and had lived together for the past two years. As the groom drank heavily, it was sad to witness this start to their marriage. Even though they had dated for ten years, they were divorced within a year. Had they thought things would change after the wedding?

There is nothing that will affect a marriage or family more profoundly than unaddressed substance misuse or mental health issues. In my career as a nurse practitioner, parenting four children, working as a Certified Prevention Specialist and as the facilitator of a peer support group for parents of substance misusing teens and young adults, I have seen marriages destroyed and families shattered. The damage can have a life-long impact on all family members.

Mental illness and substance abuse do not discriminate. They are equal opportunity, physical diseases of the brain which, if not recognized and treated, disrupt lives and destroy marriages and families. There are people who believe that these conditions are moral weaknesses or represent a lack of character. The attitude is "shape up" or "just stop." Those who work in the field of treatment, and others who take the time to read the research, know that people who suffer with alcoholism, drug addiction, depression, anxiety disorders, schizophrenia and bipolar disorder, to name a few, manifest physical changes in the brain, just as diabetics have changes in their pancreas.

Society is much more comfortable, however, talking about cancer, asthma, diabetes and hypertension. You will not see a golf tournament or a 5K race to raise money for someone suffering with addiction. Yet *all* of these are chronic, relapsing and sometimes terminal illnesses. There is the same lack of compliance regarding treatment and the same rate of relapse with all these diseases, yet they have historically been treated very differently. Why?

When we talk about behavior, as it relates to the brain, there is a stigma; a feeling that an individual has a choice with these diseases. One can certainly argue that a first drink or use of a substance was a choice, but for the genetically and bio-chemically vulnerable individual, there is little choice as the disease progresses. As a society, we have not done a good job of educating the general public about brain function and how these conditions have a biologic and genetic base. Ask anyone who suffers from them and they will not have to look far in their family tree to see a similar condition. This is not meant to provide any excuse for destructive behaviors. It is meant to recognize these diseases as a critical part of a family's medical history and illnesses that have a profound effect on relationships.

One must acknowledge a disease and take responsibility for addressing an illness, in order to get and maintain control. A diabetic needs to take responsibility for diet, weight and medication. An asthmatic needs to take responsibility for lifestyle choices, living environment and medication. A hypertensive patient needs to monitor weight, exercise, stress level and medication. Any person suffering from alcohol or drug addiction needs to recognize the effect this disease has on behavior and relationships, and take responsibility to seek counseling, attend support groups, take any needed medication and avoid substances. To expect good control and management of any of these diseases without adequate and ongoing care is unrealistic. If one believes that issues related to substance misuse or mental health will get better after marriage, or improve when the baby comes, one is courting certain heartbreak.

In these days, when you are dating and contemplating a future together, talking about your families' medical history, including substance use and mental illness, is one of the most important discussions you can have. Throw it all out on the table. If you have had issues in the past, be forthright in talking about how you have, or have not, dealt with them. How can you best support each other in addressing these concerns, so they will not lead to behaviors that will be destructive to your relationships and the lives of the children you may bring into this world? As you move on to have a family of your own, such behaviors are at high risk of recurring. If you do not have these discussions before your marriage, you can count on having them in the future. Such issues do not disappear or get better on their own.

In my role as a primary care provider, I felt a deep responsibility to ask specific questions of my patients related to their family; questions related to safety and high-risk behaviors. How are things at home? Tell me about smoking, alcohol and drug use. Do you feel safe? Are there guns at home? Are they locked up separate from the ammunition? What happens in your home when people argue? To merely perform a physical exam and not ask about the environment in which a person is living, is not providing thorough health care. The vast majority of children whom I examined were physically healthy, but many lived in homes where adult issues were contaminating the child's emotional and social development. When negative behaviors are not addressed, they often contribute to behavioral health issues for the children, as they mature into adulthood.

Many challenges you will face in your marriage are things that cannot be predicted. Others are things that can be anticipated, if you heed the warning signs and acknowledge them. Substance use, including alcohol, prescription drug use and illegal drugs, as well as gambling are among those that could and should be addressed before marriage. Even playing video games, shopping, watching sports, internet use and pornography, when taken to the extreme, can negatively impact a relationship. Reluctance or resistance to talk about such things may be the red flag signaling a problem in this area.

When your partner has free time, how is it spent? What type of activities is he or she engaged in? Do these activities take precedence over the partner and the family? Are the preferences of others given consideration and time? Even healthy hobbies, when they supersede time with spouse and family, can be a source of serious stress for a marriage. If this is a concern while you are dating, it would be naive to think things will change once you are married. As one woman put it, "his fun was always more important than my happiness, and that never changed." They divorced after two decades.

Do not wait to discuss your concerns. Take responsibility to address such things while you are dating. Remember you now have an opportunity to talk openly about the reality of your life and the future you want. Such discussions can create an emotional intimacy and trust, resulting in a partnership that provides a strong foundation for your marriage.

CHAPTER SEVENTEEN

Acknowledging Money Matters

WHEN PATRICK AND I WERE FIRST ASKED to speak with the engaged couples about finances, I chuckled to myself. Then I thought about it. Who better than us? We had been married thirty years at the time, and had made plenty of mistakes, so perhaps we would be the ideal couple to share the pitfalls to avoid. How much better it is to be educated early in your married life than learning by trial and error.

There were times in our marriage when I could have talked more openly about our sex life with less embarrassment than discussing details of our financial situation. Neither of us worked in the financial field. We had never taken any money management courses, and our parents, while modeling frugality, did not educate us about finances. Fortunately, we both were sensible with our money. We had each lived on our own before marrying and had to manage our paycheck to cover living expenses. The experience was valuable in giving us respect for the money earned and how it was spent.

Since money emerges as the number one friction leading to divorce, it is a "must discuss" topic for those in a serious relationship. It is a subject that should be addressed sooner, rather than later. During the young adult years, it is wise to live independently for a period of time to appreciate what it means to be self-supporting. Those individuals who move from their parents' home directly to living with their partner or marriage often lack the experience of budgeting, staying

65

within their income and knowing the importance of saving, all of which are best learned before joining lives.

Each of you comes into marriage with your own attitude about money. You have had different experiences growing up and watching how your parents handled finances. Who worked? Who paid the bills? How were spending and savings handled? Did you have an allowance growing up or did your parents pay for everything? Were you raised by a single mother who had to watch where every nickel went? Your grandparents may have lived through the Great Depression, so your parents witnessed the importance of being frugal. Since parents are generally the primary role model for such things, it should not be surprising that you tend to copy what you saw, unless you have made a conscious, educated decision to do otherwise.

As a teenager, can you recall how exciting it was to get that first paycheck? What did you do with it? Maybe you saved it toward buying your own car. Others may have spent it right away on a new outfit, sports equipment or the latest video game. For some, the spending was short lived, until you became a wiser consumer. For others, money could not be spent fast enough. Now as an adult, which habits do you want to emulate from your parents and your past, and which should you discard? By making conscious decisions, you can put yourself in charge of your financial future.

Contemplating marriage and joining your life with another adult means joining finances at some level. Other than extreme circumstances where there is a large amount of money, as in the case of a family trust or other obligations, a prenuptial financial agreement need not be in the initial discussion. Will you have joint accounts for everything? Will you pool money in an account for household expenses and maintain separate savings accounts? Have you discussed your financial goals to determine if you are on the same path for saving for the big purchases, like a house, a car or travel? Remember Alicia and Pete in the earlier chapter? Their inability to talk about the time frame for buying a house set them up for constant financial friction that ultimately contributed to their divorce.

You should each have a good sense of the other's spending and savings habits when you are dating. If you are a spender marrying a saver, you will need to communicate and compromise on a regular basis. You will have to figure out how best to budget your income to allow for both temperaments, while working on your long term goals. Your individual interests and hobbies will give insight as to how you each like to spend money. How will that be balanced with your mutual goals? In addition to a joint account, you may find it helpful to have separate accounts to allow some freedom to spend or save as you feel is needed. Such discussion can give insight into your partner's attitude and openness about addressing finances and the meaning that money holds.

Valuing money either too much or too little may mean a more in-depth talk or some financial counseling would be wise. You should both be willing to share your credit rating. This information will help determine if you would be better joining accounts or keeping them separate if one of you has a lower score. To join finances will bring the one of you with the better score down, rather than the reverse. It is important that you be forthright about the debt you are each carrying from your student loans, credit cards and any other financial obligations you may have.

Read financial magazines, listen to talk shows, check related online sites and talk with fiscal experts. Engage a financial counselor, if necessary, so you can be in step with each other, enjoying a smoother dance when you unpack from your honeymoon.

CHAPTER EIGHTEEN

Taking on Technology

WHEN PATRICK AND I FIRST BEGAN our work with the marriage preparation program, there were no cell phones, and computers were used only by large corporations. Recently, in a room with forty-five engaged couples, everyone had a cell phone, all of them had personal computers at home and most of them also owned laptops. We did not ask about fax machines, iPods, tablets, iPads and iPhones. We did not have to. And TVs, blu-rays and DVDs go without saying.

More families in America have five televisions in their homes, than families having only one. A twenty-something I spoke with said her dad had installed TVs into the bathrooms, now making seven in the house; he did not want to miss the news or sports. What does this mean for communication in a relationship? Maybe nothing. Maybe a lot. If you are annoyed that your partner is always checking the phone, taking calls during your time together, or texting friends when conversing with you, you are smart to address it. If you find it rude, say so now. It would be wise to get a sense where the use of technology is on your spouse's priority list, and what limits you both want to establish in your home.

Technology poses a challenge your grandparents did not have to deal with at all, your parents for only part of their adult life, but it is one that you will confront daily. You have had the internet most of your life and your children will not know life without it. It is not going away. It is growing exponentially and, in many ways, it is insidious. In our culture, it is easy not to think about its impact. Technology is just there, demanding to be addressed, but often regarded as something you have no control over. You do, however, have a say in the role that it plays; perhaps not so much in the work environment, but certainly in your home and with your family. And that is the good news.

It would give you a head start on your communication skills if you spent some time talking about the role you want technology to play in your marriage and, ultimately, your family. Not to come to some understanding and define some limits will allow a formidable intruder into your life. You both are the head and the heart of your family and can determine the climate you want in your home. When limits are not set, electronic devices can destroy intimacy, causing you to zone out others while focusing on things that, when compared to relationships, are relatively meaningless.

When the cell phone goes off, does that mean it needs to be answered? Will that text have to be checked when you and your spouse are talking—especially if the device serves as a welcome distraction in the middle of a heated discussion? Should your cell phone be shut off for awhile when you come home? Will the two of you sit for a relaxing meal and discuss the day's events, even for twenty minutes, without interruption? When children join the table will they, too, have cell phones? Will you permit this precious time to be interrupted, or will you set limits around technology during family dinner?

And then there is the question of the TV in the bedroom. Often couples do not think twice about it. They just decorate around it with all the other furnishings. I am going to suggest you leave it in the family room. Media will be pervasive in your life, both at work and at home. To leave it out of your bedroom will permit you to have one place of solitude and intimacy, where no one else is allowed. Yes, there will be some nights that you will not be happy with each other and the room will scream with silence. So be it. It is too easy to fill the void with the late night talking heads. But I will challenge you to believe that your marriage will do better in keeping that one room sacrosanct. Yes, I am saying, do not have a TV in your bedroom. I know this is a hard sell for many couples who cannot imagine not having it on when they are retiring for the night. I suggest giving it a try. You will not be sorry.

Just a word about electronic media regarding your relationship; DON'T. Do not engage in discussing or posting details for others to view. If something is problematic, you should be addressing it with each other or a counselor. Remember there is no privacy with technology. What might get you worked up one day, can blow over the next, but will forever remain for the world to see or read. Value your privacy and respect that of your partner.

Talk about technology now. It is so much easier to determine ahead of time than it is to change the rules after habits have developed. Will you two control IT or will IT control you? (Pun intended!) You decide.

CHAPTER NINETEEN

Interpreting Red Flags

BY OUR JUNIOR YEAR, one of my college friends had a serious boyfriend. Bill was handsome, personable and goal-oriented. He just adored Betsy. All our friends knew this because he was either always around or calling her on the phone. He seemed so devoted. Her family liked him too, including him in all their family events. It seemed like such a good relationship, or so we thought at the time.

One night, in particular, stands out in my mind. A few days before the end of our junior year, a group of us headed out for a girls' night at a local restaurant. We enjoyed a leisurely dinner, with lots of laughs, reminiscing about the past year. With only two semesters left, we were elated. Pulling into the dorm parking lot after dinner, one of the girls announced, "there's Bill." Guess we were not surprised, but felt a bit disappointed. Betsy was less than enthusiastic as she greeted him. She had been enjoying her evening and was not ready to have it end. "Hey, where have you been? I have been calling you and I had no idea where you were," he challenged Betsy. Those were the days before cell phones when people could not reach you any time they wanted.

Betsy and Bill married right after graduation. She became pregnant shortly thereafter. Patrick and I went to visit them when she was about three months along. We had just become engaged and were eager to share our news. I was shocked at how she had changed. Betsy's face was drawn; the sparkle had gone from her eyes. She was welcoming and happy about our engagement, but the celebratory mood was subdued. She was working as a nurse, but yearned to have a more challenging position. There was a different demeanor to her, something that seemed more than the fatigue of pregnancy, or the stress of impending motherhood. I knew Betsy and she did not seem happy.

Patrick and I married a few months later and left for our VISTA (Volunteers in Service to America) service in Texas. We did not see Betsy again for a year and a half. It was wonderful to get together with her and meet her adorable son. Bill was, as always, on the fast track of business and was not there when we visited. He worked long hours and was seldom home. This left the responsibility of parenting and the household up to Betsy. By this time, she and Bill had moved three hours away from her family. The distance, and so much time alone with a toddler, left her feeling isolated.

Bill was definitely the head of the house, making all the important decisions. Betsy was left to assume the traditional domestic role that, as a bright and energetic woman, left her feeling professionally unfulfilled. She talked with enthusiasm about nursing, yet felt frustrated at not being more involved. This absence of professional development, along with Bill's unwillingness to acknowledge its importance, seemed to leave an emptiness in Betsy. Something needed to change.

Over the next couple of years, all of us were busy living our lives: having babies, building our homes and our careers. Along with geographic distances, the pace of our lives necessitated settling for the annual Christmas card updates. Then, one year, came the news that Betsy and Bill were separating. Their families were devastated. They could not understand that Betsy's marriage was smothering her. What initially appeared as Bill's devotion had masked jealousy. His attention disguised his need to control. Betsy's individuality evaporated. Her life had become stifling. Finally, she decided to leave the marriage. Divorce was a decision she knew would have difficult repercussions within her traditional, Italian, Catholic family, but it was one she knew she had to make.

After divorcing, Betsy moved with her young son to pursue a Master's Degree in Nursing. Twelve years ago, she became CEO of a medical center, one of the few of women in the country to do so at the time. She has been recognized with numerous awards for her achievements. Betsy has been remarried for over twenty-five years to a man who respects her needs and encourages her endeavors. I share this story with the hope that you will take time to examine your relationship and listen to your inner voice, no matter how faint it may be.

Many women have felt the conflict between the domestic roles of wife and mother and those of professional interests and career demands. But recognizing red flags goes beyond working through the issues of balancing work and home. It involves identifying what is important to you; issues you can compromise on and ones which are deal breakers. Jealousy and controlling behaviors have no role in a loving, supportive partnership. Those qualities, along with Betsy's need to pursue her professional goals, and Bill's unwillingness to recognize that need, proved to be a stalemate they could not work out.

Knowing your needs and the ability to express them is critical. Listening, acknowledging and respecting your partner's feelings, provides important feedback. Can you articulate your own needs, separate from those of your spouse? Are you comfortable expressing your desires and feel they are being heard? Are you having a say in the way decisions about your life are being made? Is there dialogue that is open and respectful to both of you? The inability to compromise and arrive at a plan where both parties feel respected and valued is likely to damage a marriage beyond repair.

Over-attention may seem flattering, yet can serve to cloak jealousy. Protectiveness may camouflage the need to control. Such behaviors can become smothering and interfere with independence and personal growth. In a healthy, loving relationship, distrust and suspicion have no place. If controlling behaviors, jealousy, verbal or physical abuse are evident during your courtship, they are the crimson red flags that need attention *now*. These will not improve once you are married; often they get worse. The addition of a baby frequently escalates such problems.

In her book, *Lies at the Altar,* psychologist Dr Robin Smith poses 276 questions that provide a thorough overview of potential red flags. They are questions that over the period of dating, and talking with each other, you should be able to answer. Topics about your potential spouse's childhood, family, education, work, life experiences, past relationships, money, sex, health, parenthood, politics, friends, community involvement, social life, religion and general likes and dislikes give insight into your partner. If you have no clue about your potential spouse's attitudes and experiences in these areas, it is a good indication that more time is needed before becoming engaged.

Your gut may tell you something that your heart may not want to hear. Take the time to listen and, when in doubt, seek professional counsel. Too much happiness is at stake to leave things to chance for either of you. Taking the time for such counseling can provide the classes that will allow you to have a smoother dance if you decide to move ahead in your relationship.

CHAPTER TWENTY

Committing to Your Partner

ONE OF AMERICA'S POET LAUREATES, Robert Frost, once said, "Home is where, when you go there, they have to take you in." It should be a wonderful feeling. The commitment made in marriage should provide that same emotion, that sense of unconditional, dependable, trustworthy love.

Yes, you are entering a lawful contract with legal ramifications. Some couples look at marriage with an attitude if it does not work out we will just divorce. Such an outlook is a recipe for disaster. Marriage, like parenthood, is easy to get into and very difficult to get out of. But such a commitment has some very positive aspects, not the least of which is offering each of you a place of love and security; a place where each person can be him or herself and accepted for whom he or she is. That being the desired expectation is very likely why studies show that married people are generally healthier and live longer. They are offered better insurance rates than single people because statistics show they are more likely to be responsible, settled and stable, and therefore at less risk for accidents and injuries. Commitment can be a good thing when you are ready for it. Where do you fall on this dating continuum? Are you committed to this relationship and moving it forward?

Opposites attract, the saying goes, but they can also detract, if not pulling in the same general direction and willing to move toward compromise. Are you both on the same page? Do you have the same value system and overall goals of where you want to go? You may have different ideas on how to get there, but if you are headed in the same direction and want to be together, you have a good chance of being able to work through the bumps with heart-to-heart talks, respect and negotiation.

I am reminded of the cartoon of two mules yoked together in the middle of a field, getting very hungry. To the right was a bale of hay he was pulling toward. To the left was a bale she was pulling toward. And pull they did, until they both broke down in exhaustion and ultimately starved. They both wanted and needed the same thing, but their unwillingness to plan together and compromise prevented them from sauntering over and eating one bale together and then, when hungry again, heading over to the other bale, committed and satisfied. Instead, they starved each other to death. Some couples do that to their marriage.

I was working with a third-year female medical resident who told me that she met her husband in California. She was a nanny at the time and he was a nurse. She was contemplating going to nursing school, but he encouraged her to go to medical school. She took all the prerequisite courses and then applied; not at all sure she would get accepted. When she did, it meant moving to the Midwest, a far cry from sunny California. After finishing medical school, she needed to complete a residency, and they hoped to return to California. As luck would have it, she got accepted to an Ivy League school on the East Coast, taking them even farther away from home. As she was nearing the end of her residency, she was offered the opportunity to stay on and become Chief Resident the following year. Therefore, instead of leaving in ten months and returning to the West Coast, there would be an additional year in New England. Although she was honored to be asked, and knowing it would be a great resume builder, she was aware of the sacrifices her husband had already made.

"He has supported me through all this. I wouldn't expect anything more," she said to me. So she presented it to him for the final decision, "I will only ask you once and I will never bring it up again; do you want to stay for another year, for me to do this?" He responded affirmatively and they planned to move to California after she completed her year as Chief. A plan is made with discussion, support and compromise; no ultimatums, give and take. This is a good example of marital collaboration that allows for an easier, smoother dance.

Like this couple, many circumstances will come up that no one can predict when you embark on married life. Having a sense of what to expect is important. Enter marriage with your eyes wide open. Are you willing to make the commitment to stay on for the ride, to wherever it takes you? If you both agree that divorce is not an option, it simplifies a lot of decisions you will face together. Is your relationship one of similar values and goals, strong love, sincere caring for the welfare of the other, with the willingness to be flexible? If those ingredients are present, there is likely to be a smoother dance with a happy outcome for you both.

CHAPTER TWENTY-ONE

Engaging in Your Future

"WE'RE ENGAGED!" The happy announcement brings forth the expected best wishes and congratulatory responses. It is amazing how a simple ring on the finger can change everything. Endless discussions of reception halls, attendants, flowers, music and the rehearsal dinner dominate the couple's conversation, along with the other details requiring decisions over the upcoming months. In the midst of the wedding planning frenzy, many a couple has wondered what happened to those fun-filled weekends and quiet evenings.

The demands of this time may serve to emphasize the importance of addressing the issues raised in the previous chapters, before engagement. With the details of "the wedding" dominating everything, there is precious little time to do so now. The financial commitment involved in the contracts for the occasion adds additional stress. Discovering conflicts at this stage could derail the event, resulting in a costly outcome, both emotionally and financially. This is why rushing to this stage is never a good idea. When engaged couples are within weeks, even months, of getting married, it is a challenge raising topics that should have been addressed previously. Giving each other the gift of time is a precious gift indeed.

When planning a wedding, there is much opportunity for discussion and compromise. Respecting a budget (regardless who is paying), and making decisions about location, number of guests, seating arrangements and menu, as well as deciding on the honeymoon, will be great practice for the future. If the details of planning this event are causing frequent blow-ups, it is time to ask, "What is this telling us?" When the attention on the wedding is causing more continuous friction than fun, then something is seriously out of balance. Are you investing time in the most important aspect of your special day, the wedding ceremony? Are you giving equal thought to your vows and readings, so they reflect the love and commitment you are making?

Your wedding should be a joyous occasion to commemorate your commitment to each other, shared with family and friends. The reception should be a celebration you will enjoy and remember, long after it is over. But your wedding *is* a one day event. What happens after that, is the rest of your life; your marriage. Couples who can keep that perspective do not experience the post wedding let-down, because they are looking forward to their future. The anticipation of building your life together, your home, careers and family over the years ahead, should provide much to look forward to after the wedding.

II

"The Tango"

THE EARLY YEARS OF MARRIAGE

*"The most important thing in any relationship is not
what you get, but what you give."*

—Eleanor Roosevelt

"The Tango"

When you get beyond the "Bunny Hop" and move on to marriage, you will likely find your dance has morphed into the "Tango." These early years of marriage can be viewed as the passionate period with many different versions of the Tango; some emphasize the close upper body embrace that allows for fancy footwork and twirling. Other versions display the close contact in the pelvis and upper thighs. Regardless of the variations, one could agree that the "Tango" is a dance that displays both dramatic and passionate elements.

During this dance you feel confident, sure of yourself and your partner. You are soul mates, very hungry for each other's presence, physically and emotionally. This is a lively period and, although the intensity will change, the passion need not evaporate. This is an especially critical time because habits are being formed in your marriage. Healthy habits can cement the strong foundation needed to withstand the obstacles life will throw onto your dance floor.

Learning to keep some steps of the "Tango" alive in your relationship can make the difference in a marriage that not only survives, but thrives. This is an important stage to establish habits. These are the behaviors that will get you through life's inevitable challenges. The important thing to remember is that no stage is perfect, and no stage is without its delights. For now, tango the night away!

CHAPTER TWENTY-TWO

Constructing the Marriage Table

SOME COUPLES SEEM TO VIEW MARRIAGE as something that just "happens." Maybe such an attitude reflects the demise of so many relationships. The truth is that a long term, satisfying marriage takes effort. That does not mean it is to be viewed as a painstaking project. In fact, marriage should be looked at as a lifestyle one willingly chooses as the basis for happiness in adulthood. It is the foundation on which one builds a family, a career and one's physical, emotional, financial, social, sexual and spiritual life. Best not to leave that to chance!

Let's picture marriage as a construction project, like building a table. Some small decorative tables have one leg, with a small tripod foot at its base. As an accent piece, they are usually found in the corner of the room holding a small plant or picture. Other tables have two pedestal type legs, each with tripod feet, as seen in some dining room tables, like the Duncan Phyfe style. Others have three separate legs secured to the wood to provide equal balance. The more traditional tables providing sturdy, multi-purpose use have four legs positioned one on each corner, assuring that this table will not easily collapse. Viewing marriage as a long and broad piece of wood you want to make into a sturdy table will help you think about what legs you want to install. The decision as to how many legs you will put under your table may vary depending on the stage of your marriage and the circumstances you face.

If you concentrate on building at least four strong pillars, you will find that your table can withstand quite a bit of turmoil. There will be those times when more stress is put on it and a few extra legs are needed. When one spouse has a health challenge, a job is lost, a parent dies, a child is sick, mental illness or substance misuse occurs with a family member, these things can tip your table pretty dramatically. The sturdiest of tables is going to need added support during these times. Recognizing this can make the critical difference in getting the help you need. But like anything else, preparation is the key. Build your marriage strong to begin with and add other legs as needed. Let's think about what legs should be considered for basic stability.

LEGS OF SUPPORT

RESPECT is an attribute that goes a long way in stabilizing a marriage. You and your spouse may differ in your opinions on issues, but when you respect your spouse as a person, you can then compromise with each other and not feel the need to dictate all decisions. Respect is the basis of a healthy partnership.

LOVE provides a strong leg. The ability to express your love to each other through words and small acts of kindness (a quick neck rub or spontaneous hug) can get you through a lot of things that might otherwise tip your table. You can be really upset with your spouse for any number of reasons, but if the love is there, it will give you the reason to come back together and deal with the issues.

SPIRITUALITY can provide a strong leg of support to a partnership. A belief in God or the acknowledgement of a Higher Power has been shown to offer additional strength to a marriage, especially in times of stress. You may not practice the same religion, but having a strong spiritual base to your life will offer solid reinforcement to your marriage.

Constructing the Marriage Table

TRUST is a critical pillar of a relationship. Sexual fidelity is the essence of trust and provides integrity to your marriage. Such commitment to each other allows emotional and psychological intimacy to grow and thrive. Financial fidelity is also a form of trust that affords security to your relationship.

These are four legs to install under your marriage table. Take time to talk about these and the role you see them playing in your marriage. What other legs do you feel are important to solidify your relationship? For example, you might want to build in a sense of humor. That leg can add levity and stability to a marriage. The ability to laugh at oneself, and with your spouse, can reduce stress in addressing difficult issues. A well placed one-liner can calm an eruption, where anything else might prove to be unproductive. The more legs you can add, the more you strengthen your marriage and the less likely your table will be easily up-ended or collapse altogether.

CHAPTER TWENTY-THREE

Respecting vs. Understanding

AN EXERCISE I USE WITH ENGAGED COUPLES is to ask them to think about a couple whose marriage reflects the kind of relationship they would like for themselves. I then ask them to identify what qualities this couple displays they most admire. They have been given a small card to write down the one word descriptions. One attribute that inevitably comes up is "understanding." It serves to remind me that, however important this trait is, it can be a challenge, even in the best of relationships.

Some issues that will arise in your marriage will be a source of frustration that you will never understand; like my expecting Patrick would be handy with projects around the house. Because his father and his brother were clever, and I erroneously believed every male is handy, I expected him to fall right in line. Watch out for stereotypes and preconceived expectations. Patrick does not enjoy handyman activities. I just could not understand it. So I had to ask myself, how important is this going to be in the happiness of my marriage? Am I going to allow it to be an ongoing source of frustration?

I finally came to appreciate that gardening was his forte. His efforts have beautified our home more than other projects that held no interest for him. I learned to adopt the motto "do it yourself, or pay someone else" and I finally accepted it. When I look at the card I had written out on the values I admire, I had never listed "handyman." But the qualities I did list are ones I cannot pay someone for, and are the ones I have come to respect and cherish.

There are things that you are never going to understand about your spouse. Some of the differences will be more serious than my handyman example. To begin with, you are different people: from gender, personalities, upbringings, childhood and life experiences, to name but a few. To expect that you will always understand your spouse's reactions or views on certain subjects is unrealistic. To recognize the difference between the issues that are frustrating and those that will be deal breakers is critical. Experiencing frustration is one thing, losing respect for your partner signals the demise of a marriage.

The small index cards the couples are given for this exercise are cut the size of a credit card to fit neatly into their wallets. This card represents the values that each has identified as representing a good marriage. Do this for yourself. Write down attributes that you feel are important, and are ones you wish to emulate in your own relationship. This can serve as a useful reminder. The card is likely to fall out unexpectedly one day when the credit card is used. If you left the house that morning with a hurtful remark and see the word "respect" staring at you, you may be apt to think more seriously about your behavior. Such a tool can provide a helpful roadmap, as you each reflect on those qualities you have deemed important in a strong and loving relationship.

While attempts at understanding your spouse will not always be easy, respect for your spouse is critical to your marriage. I may not understand why Patrick has an aversion to handy work, but it is important for me to respect his feelings. Feelings are not right or wrong, good or bad; they are personal. A healthy marriage, like any relationship, must be based on respect. Respect will always trump understanding.

CHAPTER TWENTY-FOUR

Dealing with Parents and In-Laws

AMONG THE TOP FOUR STRESSORS in a marriage is the relationship with in-laws. Unlike the other three stressors, money, sex and religion, this one involves third and fourth parties. And not just any party, but the ones who, for better or worse, have had the most impact on you and your spouse's lives. Remember, these people reared the person you have chosen to spend the rest of your life with and both the positive and negative effects will, forever, have a bearing on your marital relationship. Stress from in-laws can contribute to a marriage ending in divorce. Prevention calls for some ground rules.

I have heard it said, "Take a good look at your partner's family; you are marrying them too." Many couples will attest to this being true. An earlier chapter, "Reflecting on the Family of Origin" encourages you to take note of this, as it will have a bearing on your marriage. Even if you do not live geographically close to your in-laws, their influence will be felt by you and your spouse, and in your marriage. The exciting thing for you both is that you no longer have to live under the dictates of your parents, but now have the freedom to define what you want for yourself, your spouse, and your married life. This freedom can be a positive and exhilarating experience. The sooner you establish this independence, the less conflict will occur between the two of you and with your parents and in-laws.

How will your holidays be spent? This is an area where

in-laws can add stress to a marriage. It can be minimized, however, if you can get a sense of this and discuss it early on. One example we talk about with the couples is to make a pact never to make promises to one's parents without first talking to your spouse. It can catch you off guard, if you do not agree ahead of time to consult before offering an answer. Like leaving one in-law's house around Halloween and the mother says, "We'll see you at Thanksgiving, right?" If you just matter-of-factly respond "sure, Mom," you are in for an adventurous ride home! A better response would be, "Gee, Mom, thanks for the invitation. We haven't talked about the holidays yet. Let me get back to you next week." Such a response is respectful to all parties, but noncommittal. It also sets the tone that things are different now. You two are your own family. It may shock, even sadden Mom at first, but hopefully, she will get over it.

If you are familiar with the television sitcom *Everyone Loves Raymond*, you only need to change Ray's mother's hair color and add an Irish lilt and you will have a fairly good picture of my beloved mother-in-law, Molly. Raymond's character was a classic example of a man who never cut the apron strings, often intimidated and manipulated by his perfect homemaker-mother, "Marie Barrone." This was written, of course, as a terrifically funny sitcom and the lines were delivered perfectly. It gave an all too realistic portrayal of the very real and harmful stress in-laws can cause. Fortunately, for me, Patrick was far more supportive and assertive than Raymond, when it came to issues that arose between his mother and me.

We were married for 31 years before we lost my mother-in-law, at age eighty-eight. I can recall having only one minor confrontation with her, and that was when Patrick was absent from the room. There were likely several reasons she and I did not experience more frequent conflicts. Certainly living one hundred thirty-five miles apart played a role (unlike

Marie who lived across the street and frequently walked in on Raymond and Debra!) Not having regular contact with my in-laws meant that visits were less frequent and more special. There was never a question in my mind that Patrick gets the major credit for smooth sailing in the in-law department. He always stepped in.

I never doubted my mother-in-law's love and appreciation for me, but her way of addressing situations, when they did not match her standards, was startlingly direct, softened only by her disarming brogue. Sometimes her comments were so cleverly phrased they could slide over my head, before slamming me on the backside! Like the time she and my father-in-law were visiting and she opened the fridge to get something. Lingering for a few seconds to survey the interior, she then commented to my father-in-law, "That reminds me, Jack, when we get home, I need to clean the refrigerator." Now one might surmise that mine was so sparkling that it was in direct contrast to her fridge. Let me assure you that was never the case! She epitomized the spotless housecleaner. On my best day, I am casual. Before I could even process her comment, Patrick responded with, 'What did you mean by that, Mom?" After she muddled through some response on the state of her own fridge, he concluded with, "Oh good, because I am sure you would not be insinuating that ours is not clean." And so it went.

Patrick would call his mother to task when she made any comment that might be construed as insulting or critical to me, or to our household. Whenever she made a remark that could be viewed as demeaning, he respectively, but firmly, clarified it on the spot. I felt so supported I could move past it and enjoy her many redeeming and loving qualities. After all, I only needed to remind myself that she did raise a son who is a good and loving husband and I thanked her for that on many occasions. What better accolade can a mother receive?

Patrick provides an important lesson for married couples, and one that newlyweds would be wise to institute from the get-go: Your first responsibility is to your spouse. While it is important to be loving and respectful to one's parents, it is essential to be loyal to each other first. When issues arise or comments are made that are critical or undermining to your mate, you must lovingly, but firmly, intervene. Doing this early on can prevent hurt and discord and set a supportive tone for your marriage.

Your spouse is the person you are sharing your life with now, and with whom you are building a family. In the natural course of life, your marriage will outlive your in-laws. If you allow cracks to erupt that leave your spouse feeling hurt and inadequate, you will, in the end, be the victim of your mate's destroyed self esteem. Stick up for each other. Such loyalty will reap huge benefits for both of you in your marriage, and keep your dance much smoother.

CHAPTER TWENTY-FIVE

Fostering Spirituality in Marriage

MAYBE WHEN YOU SAW THE TITLE of this chapter, you were tempted to skip it. Perhaps you thought, "Is this going to be about attending a service every Sunday and getting involved with a church?" It would be great if spirituality in marriage was that easy!

Spirituality is not something you do; it is something you are, to each other. It is the day-to-day living together where true spirituality resides and that which requires the most work. It is the life, energy and enthusiasm that you infuse into your relationship. It is what makes your marriage alive. The very word "enthusiasm" came from the Greek word "enthousiasmos," meaning to be inspired. Is that what you are demonstrating? When others are in your company, are they inspired? Do they feel better about themselves when they are with you? Is your glass half full or half empty? The half-empty glass represents someone who saps the energy out of a relationship. We all know people who expect others to pump them up every time you are with them, like the high maintenance temperament written about in an earlier chapter. What are you bringing to your marriage? Are you accountable for infusing some positive energy into your relationship or do you expect your spouse to be responsible for your happiness?

The opportunities you will have to instill spiritual strength into your relationship will not be found in grandiose moments. They will be found in the mundane. How do you greet your spouse when you arrive home from a stressful day at work? Do you pull the "kick the cat" routine? That is when you walk in the house with all the frustrations from work and kick the cat when it crosses your path. That is an example of displaced anger. Many of us do that to our spouse, figuratively speaking. He or she is not to blame, but yet become the repository of our bad mood and the target of our frustrations. A healthier way is to recognize where your agitations originate and deal with them accordingly. Two good maxims are: "Deal with work at work" and "Deal with your family issues at home." Neither is responsible for the other. It will simplify your life.

Uninterrupted time alone every day with your spouse ensures that regular communication is built into your marriage. Planning for a regular family dinner time is a way of connecting daily with your spouse and children. If business travel prevents these events from happening in person, "Skyping" family dinner and a having a late night phone conversation with your spouse can provide a substitute until you can connect face to face. It is the prioritizing of such events that makes the difference.

Learn not to take your spouse for granted. Have you ever noticed how some people treat others better than they do a loved one? Do you talk to your husband/wife in a way that you would not dream of talking to your neighbor or co-worker? One of the simplest ways to elevate the spirituality of your marriage is to be nice to your spouse. Remember basic manners: the "please" and the "thank you," the offers of help, doing things without being asked. Sounds simple, doesn't it? Do not mistake simple for easy. It is not. But it will raise the vibrancy of your relationship.

Sexual intimacy is the height of the spirituality of marriage, when it is based on fidelity. Being faithful to each other is the cornerstone of a healthy, loving, growing, spiritual marriage. Allowing the time and space for physical intimacy should be a priority. Keep the bedroom a space that is free from the interference of technology. Having soothing music and lighting can provide a welcome retreat after a stressful day. Even on those days when you may not feeling particularly amorous, such an atmosphere can soothe your souls, allowing for emotional intimacy.

The holiness of your marriage will be challenged by daily stresses. Jobs are demanding and traveling and commuting are tiring. Financial challenges can be a huge factor in a marriage, as you work to pay the bills, knock off the debt of student loans and credit cards, save for emergencies, the children's college fund and retirement, all while you try to support charities and have some left for fun. For most couples, it is a real juggling act and not surprising that money is the number one marital problem. Your ability to deal with these stresses, without turning every discussion into a heated argument, will be aided by the spirituality you infuse into your relationship.

If spirituality is thought to be the breath and life of your marriage, you want to nurture it, not destroy it. One way to do that is through prayer, and not the kind of formal prayer recited in church. I am referring here to solitude; a rare thing for many people today and often unknown to married couples. Solitude is that designated fifteen minutes a day where you seek quiet. You shut out the world of auditory chaos, calm your mind and center yourself. Solitude allows for inner prayer where you can have a conversation with God that involves both talking and listening. Give the gift of solitude to each other every day. It is amazing what this can do to smooth out your marriage dance.

Remember in my opening comments I said that going to church would be simple. The effort to attend a weekly church service can pale by comparison with how you live your daily life. The routine of everyday living and how you treat each other is the true essence of spirituality in your marriage. Periodically, it is good to ask yourself the question "what is it like to be married to me?" Ponder the answer. Then adjust your dance steps accordingly.

CHAPTER TWENTY-SIX

Insulating Your Marriage

THERE WILL BE PEOPLE IN YOUR LIFE that will not be a positive influence on your marriage. Sadly, these may be individuals whom you love and may be connected to, like family members or old college friends. But now, as a married couple, they may not be an asset to your relationship. Perhaps they are one of those high maintenance people referred to earlier. Maybe it is a couple who bickers, and often criticizes each other. When you are alone with them, they talk about the flaws in their mate. Over time, you may find yourself focusing on your mate's shortcomings. This is as much a virus as is the flu. The vaccine is avoidance. Minimize the time and intimate conversations you have with these people.

Do not be a spouse who talks about the aggravations of your partner with friends and co-workers. What is to be gained? They cannot do anything about the issue. Instead, they are learning negative things about your spouse that, long after you have worked them through, they will not forget. Be protective of your partner. Keep negative conversation about your spouse between the two of you, a counselor and God. To do otherwise is a form of, what I refer to as, emotional infidelity. It is destructive to the intimacy of a marriage.

Quite the opposite, saying nice things about your spouse to others, complimenting your spouse in front of others, goes a long way in fostering loving feelings. I certainly have been taken aback when a relative stranger, like a teller where we bank or a store clerk whose business we frequent will say,

"Oh, your husband always talks so nicely about you. You are so lucky. Most husbands don't do that." It certainly encourages me to overlook petty aggravations, and be grateful for the kindness Patrick has expressed about me to others.

At times of frustration, try to focus on why you married your spouse. Let those strengths overshadow the shortcomings. Give your mate something to live up to by empowering him or her. Show affection by writing a note, come home with flowers or tickets to a game or concert. Expressing gratitude in your life has an amazing effect on a person. Counting your blessings can help minimize your frustrations, and is a daily expression of love. Such actions have an incredible effect on your dance routine. Try it!

CHAPTER TWENTY-SEVEN

"Love, at its Best, is Giving What You Need to Get"

I FORGET WHEN THESE WORDS first popped into my head, but I do know it was in the very early years of our marriage. I suspect it occurred when I was lamenting something that my neophyte husband did not do for me. Memory escapes me, but I undoubtedly expected Patrick to know that "the something" was important to me. Of course, I had never told him that. We did not have the advantage of years together that might have even offered the hope of his knowing such a thing about me.

After a few more similar blunders, I realized that this kind-hearted man did not think like I did. I began to notice things that upset him were not even on my radar screen. Gradually, however, I realized that often our needs had some basic similarities: like the need for unconditional love, recognition of the good things that we each did, the overlooking of minor mistakes, the need for encouragement, not criticism, and the longing for a spontaneous hug.

Did you ever notice how easily you can focus on your spouse *not* meeting your needs and complain about all his or her irritating traits? With little effort you can go on a tirade about everything that is wrong. Yet, chronic complaining rarely changes things for the better. And is not "better" what you are looking for? If you want your needs met, you first have to know what they are. Secondly, you need to figure out which ones you can and should be meeting on your own. Are you expecting your spouse to solve problems that you could find solutions to without it turning into a major conflict?

For many women, one chief complaint often heard is, "He doesn't help me enough around the house. I have to do everything. I work full time too." Fair enough. Studies have shown that when women were home full time they did 84% of the household chores. Now that they work full time, outside the home, they do 76%. So it is often a real issue that needs to be faced. The way in which it is addressed, however, can make the critical difference in whether it ends with a solution, a compromise, or continues as an ongoing source of conflict.

One thing that has helped couples, is to state the problem ONCE. (That can be a challenge for some of us women!) Then, focus on solutions. "I am feeling overwhelmed by all the things that need to be done in the house; laundry, dishes, cleaning, vacuuming, grocery shopping and cooking. I find myself annoyed and frustrated. I do not like feeling like that and I know it's no fun for you either. I'd like for us to have more time together in the evening, and on the weekends, to enjoy each other and do things together. Could we come up with some ideas about addressing the household chores that could make that happen?"

Defining the problem once and then turning the focus on possible solutions diverts the conversation from one of chronic complaining. We all hate to be nagged. It tends to make us defensive, which creates an argumentative cycle, with increasing tension and no solution to the problem. If you find yourselves confronting the same issue repeatedly, then you want to look at what is not being addressed. Brainstorm. What could make the situation easier for both of you? Are there some areas where your spouse could use some help, where he or she is feeling stressed? It usually is not one-sided. When needs go unrecognized or unacknowledged, resentment is inevitable. If not addressed, such resentment can fester like an unhealed wound.

It is rarely one cataclysmic event that destroys a marriage. It is much more often an accumulation of unmet needs that results in the death of emotional intimacy. If you can articulate your own desires and show your spouse love, care and concern, you are much more likely to see that behavior reciprocated. The ability to identify your needs and acknowledge those of your spouse is likely to result in less stepping on toes and a smoother dance for both of you.

CHAPTER TWENTY-EIGHT

Speaking the Language of Love

IN HIS BOOK, *THE FIVE LOVE LANGUAGES*, Gary Chapman refers to learning the "language" of "quality conversations" as similar to learning a foreign language. If you can remember back to your first high school exposure to Spanish or French, you may recall understanding the teacher before you ever felt confident to attempt speaking aloud in class. Succeeding at achieving emotional intimacy in your marriage will require insight and new skills and, like any new skill, will require practice.

Mr. Chapman refers to the Minimal Daily Requirements (MDR) for "quality conversation." He suggests talking about three events that happened to you today and how you felt about them (being careful not to talk about what you did or said, but rather how you FELT about what occurred.) This often does not come naturally for most couples, but with about three weeks of practice, conversation can flow more easily. Such dialogue increases the emotional intimacy within a relationship.

In the chapter on "Noting Your Personality Differences," the challenge of the introvert and extrovert learning to dance in rhythm was addressed. The family in which you were raised had a culture of communication. Perhaps, they were loud and boisterous, no topic was off limits. Dinnertime was rambunctious. Often, however, children grow up in households where difficulties were not acknowledged openly; displays of emotions were not encouraged. You may have learned to keep any sadness to yourself or were punished when showing anger. The message such an environment teaches is to keep your feelings under wrap. Deal with them on your own. Then you get married and suddenly you are supposed to be the great communicator. How does that work? Pretty poorly, if you are not open to learning new skills.

When you can recognize what your primary emotional needs are, you can then express them to your spouse with the hope that there will be attempts to meet them. Likewise, when your spouse is able to share with you his or her needs, you, too, can make a genuine effort to meet those wishes. Since such needs are often different, it will require you to think outside the box. What your spouse desires may not be a personal need for you at all. So it will require you to do some things differently to fill those wants for your partner. Reflecting on the first chapter of this book, "Knowing Yourself," the importance of knowing and recognizing your moods and emotions can help this conversation.

But, therein lies the difference between marriages that are thriving, and not merely surviving. Chapman recognizes five love languages: *appreciation, quality time, receiving gifts, acts of service and physical touch*. I think his description of how to fill your own "love tank" and that of your spouse can make a critical difference in a marriage. Sometimes you do not know what your primary need is, but, once discovered, it can help to improve the emotional intimacy of a relationship. These needs may shift during the life-span, but knowing what your needs are at a given time, can certainly enrich a marriage.

I remember, early in our marriage, winning a silly $5 bet about a song title. When Patrick came home from errands into our 3rd floor, 3 room apartment, he had a small bouquet of flowers with a five dollar bill stapled around the stems. How classy was that?! My heart melted. Over time, the occasional flowers were accompanied by a note. I came to treasure the notes more than the flowers. With the addition of children and more rooms to clean, I could get turned on by Patrick doing housework. And now anytime a back scratch is offered, it is a trip to Shangri La! So I guess my love language has shifted over time, but the "love tank" has never hit empty.

Patrick has let me know that time spent together is one of his needs, and one of his greatest joys. And I would say that appreciation shown to each other has been important for both of us. Since men's work, historically, has been played out in the work place, it has often been taken for granted. Women, historically, have been multi-tasking the mundane chores at home. And that, too, is often taken for granted. As women have returned to the work place, they have often felt frustrated about all the remaining housework. As more demands have been expected of men at home, they have often felt under-appreciated for the domestic tasks they are now expected to assume. This shift has caused friction and dissatisfaction in many marriages. It would seem that reflecting on these "love languages" could serve to revitalize and re-energize marriages during these very busy years. Knowing what your own needs are will allow you to inform your spouse. This communication is an ongoing process, as those needs often change during different phases of your life. Keeping each other's "love tank" replenished will help keep both of you dancing in sync.

CHAPTER TWENTY-NINE

Prioritizing Tea Time

FOR THE MANY YEARS OF OUR MARRIAGE, tea time has had a revered place in our daily routine. Growing up, I do not remember tea being served, except to calm my stomach when I was home ill as a child. But marrying into an Irish family (Patrick was born on St. Patrick's Day in Belfast, Northern Ireland!) his mother prided herself on presenting the perfect pot of tea. I came to look upon it as a welcoming and cozy ritual; the kind of feeling I wanted to permeate our home.

One of the first wedding gifts we received was a whistling tea kettle. It was as loud as a steam engine chugging full bore up a mountainside. Some people might find that sound obnoxious. To me, it represented the call to calmness. It heralded a special time with Patrick, where we would block out the world and sit together. After the children arrived, tea time followed the chaos of bedtime. Later, when the children could mind themselves safely, we hosted our tea time in the living room, when Patrick arrived home from work. The children scattered to other parts of the house. They came to respect this as a sacred time that they did not interrupt.

The children are now grown and out of the home, but the tea kettle steams on. We have burned out many kettles, but my mother-in-law's little brewing pot still stands as a testament to the importance of tea. Tea time has remained a focal point in our household, especially as technology threatened to encroach on our lives. This is a time when we know we can silence the cell phone, ignore the texting, turn off the fax and instead look at each other and ask, "How was your day?" and know there will be uninterrupted time for an answer. When the now young adults come home for a visit, within ten minutes of arrival, they ask for a cup of tea. I know that shared cup of tea has come to represent, for them also, the call to calmness and the comfort of home.

Consider tea time as an example of a habit you can establish early in your marital dance routine. What ritual can you build into your daily life that will keep you emotionally connected? Such consistency can provide stability that sustains a marriage through the inevitable ups and downs which occur in every relationship. For now, focus on discovering those steps that allow you to stay in sync and remain on top of your dance.

"How do you keep the music playing?"
Song by James Ingram

How do you keep the music playing?
How do you make it last?
How do you keep the song from fading
too fast?

If we can be the best of lovers,
Yet be the best of friends,
If we can try with every day to make it better as it grows,
With any luck, then I suppose,
The music never ends.

Epilogue

PATRICK TELLS THE ENGAGED COUPLES that it would be nice if marriage was one straight shot to nirvana. Instead, it is more like a ride on the "Wild Mouse" roller coaster, having to hold on through every turn. But when that ride is over there is an exhilaration and pride at having survived. Giving serious consideration, during your dating years, to the qualities that you deem important increases the likelihood that your choice of a spouse will be done thoughtfully.

Establishing healthy habits in the first years of your relationship can prevent the chronic missteps that too many marriages experience. Attending to your relationship, with the same respect you afford you career and the energy you invest in buying a car, is likely to result in a life-long and emotionally satisfying marriage. Together you can learn to recognize challenges when they arise and not allow them to fester. You gain confidence knowing that you can weather the storms and come out the other side.

As you progress into the middle years of your marriage, there will be circumstances that add to the complexity of your relationship. The habits that you have established during the early stages will be the ones that will serve you in the years ahead. The dance steps you learn early in your journey can ensure you will be there for "The Waltz." The joys and challenges of the middle years of "Line Dancing," "Twist and Shout" and "The Cha-Cha" will be addressed in the sequel. For now, I hope this book has motivated you to establish healthy habits early that will keep you on the dance floor.

—Susan McKeown APRN, CPS

Resources

BOOKS

Briggs-Myers, Isabel and Peter B. Myers, *Gifts Differing: Understanding Personality Types*

Chapman, Gary, *The Five Love Languages*

Fertel, Mort, *Marriage Fitness*

Gottman, John, Ph.D. with Nan Silver, *The Seven Principles for Making Marriage Work*

Gottman, John, Ph.D. and Nan Silver, *What Makes Love Last?*

Gottman, John, Ph.D. and Nan Silver, *Why Marriages Succeed or Fail*

Gray, John *Men are from Mars, Women are from Venus*

Haag, Pamela, *Marriage Confidential*

Hendrix, Harville, Ph.D. *Getting the Love You Want*

Littauer, Florence, *Personality Plus*

Olson, Suzanne, *I Hate Financial Planning*

Orman, Suzie, *The 9 Steps to Financial Freedom*

Schnarch, Ph.D. *Passionate Marriage*

Smith, Robin Dr. *Lies at the Altar*

MAGAZINES

Consumer Reports Magazine

Kiplingers Personal Finance Magazine

Money Magazine

ONLINE

Center for Marital and Family Studies at the University of Denver

Jay, Meg, Ph.D., the Defining Decade: "Why Your Twenties Matter" (2012)

Myers-Briggs Personality Assessment

National Center for Health Statistics / National Survey of Family Growth

People Mapping Personality Assessment, Dr. Michael Lillibridge

The National Marriage Project, University of Virginia

The Wedding Report. Inc. / The Wedding Report.com

About the Author

SUSAN MCKEOWN, APRN, CPS, is a graduate of St. Anselm College with a B.S. degree in Nursing, and Northeastern University's Pediatric Nurse Practitioner Program. She worked with families as a nurse practitioner for over forty years. Susan is a Certified Prevention Specialist, educating and advocating on issues of mental health and substance misuse. For the past eleven years she has co-facilitated a weekly support group for parents whose children, teens and young adults have substance issues.

Susan lives with her husband in New Hampshire where they have conducted seminars for engaged couples for four decades.